Happy cooking!

Harris Golden

Golden's Kitchen

19.95

THE ARTISTRY OF
COOKING AND DINING
ON THE LIGHT SIDE

HARRIS GOLDEN

EXECUTIVE CHEF
ELIZABETH ARDEN'S MAINE CHANCE

Library of Congress Catalog Number 85-063467
ISBN 0-930380-19-3

Quail Run books are published by
Quail Run Publications, Inc.
2705 East Indian School Road
Phoenix, Arizona 85016

Trademark registered with the
United States Patent Office

Printed in U.S.A.

Quail
Run

To Sandy, Darren, Brad and Tyler, too,
who cheerfully surrendered so many hours
to the making of this book,
and to my mother
who inspired me with her wonderful cooking.

My sincerest appreciation and thanks to the following people:

Sandy, my wife, co-photographer and co-illustrator,
whose devotion and constant support have been invaluable.

Shelly Dessen for her discriminating eye and
taste-buds-on-duty twenty-four hours a day.

Dorothy Powers, R.D. for her excellent nutritional advice.

Dr. Mitchel Lipton for his critique on the
beginning stages of the cookbook project.

Dr. Francis W. Price, director of industrial medicine for Eli Lilly and Company,
who was my first source of encouragement in the writing of this book.

Joan Nagy, the editorial director for Hearst Books,
who was my last source of encouragement.

Linda Vaughn, PhD, Dept. of Nutrition, Arizona State University,
for her critique on the diet philosophy.

Anthony Dolphin, the sous chef and backbone of the Maine Chance kitchen,
for many years of hard work and devotion to all my endeavors.

Frederick Quirk, Maine Chane General Manager,
with whom it is an honor to work.

Jennifer Wilkins and Dawn Turner who make my day so much easier
and so much brighter.

Diane Jones for her constant encouragement and support.

Tod Hurst for his humorous and accurate criticisms on new dishes devised.

Darlene Hartkopf who transformed a poorly typed manuscript into a legible one.

Noreen Estfan, Felicia Oram, Jaci Young, Mary Hawkins and John Long
who helped me transform the manuscript into this beautiful book.

The late Barney Kroll who believed in me and gave me the helm of my first
commercial kitchen to grow up in prior to my twenty-first birthday.

Finally, special thanks to the Maine Chance guests
and the students from the Smiling Gourmet Cooking School
for the many years of devotion and encouragement.

Contents

Apple-Orange Punch
Baer's Eggs in Casserole
(baked eggs with vegetables, sausage and sherry)
Braided French Bread

Cranapple Nedlogs
*(crepes filled with ricotta cheese, dates and pecans,
served with cranapple sauce and fresh fruit)*

Botanical Fruit
Three Cheese Omelet
High-Figer Bran Muffins

Fresh Orange Juice
Amaretto Buttermilk Pancakes
*(garnished with coconut, walnuts and raisins,
served with maple syrup, raspberries and yogurt)*

Hot Apple Cider with Cinnamon
Spinach, Cheese and Mushroom Frittata
Soy Flour Corn Muffins

Contents

Contents

Contents

Contents

Contents

Contents

Contents

★ see An Important Word About the Menus and Recipes, page 15

RELATED READING

Introduction

To this day I can recall the dread which overcame me in sixth grade when all students were measured for height and weight. Knowing what was to come, as the nurse called roll loud and clear, I sat at my desk sweating and waiting. "John Denato -- height, fifty-six inches -- weight, seventy-eight pounds; Anthony Depasquali -- height, sixty-one inches -- weight, a hundred and one pounds; Harris Golden --height, sixty inches -- weight, a hundred fifty-five pounds."

As had happened before, laughter filled the classroom and, shame-facedly stepping off the scale, I wanted time to stop. I wanted everything to cease existing.

I wanted not to be fat! But food was a popular subject at home. My mother was an excellent cook, so mealtime was always a pleasurable experience and more than fulfilling.

I was growing up with mixed emotions. I loved to eat, I felt guilty eating, and I hated being fat. Food, which I found so enjoyable, was turning into my worst enemy. It didn't make sense, so I began to look for my own solution.

My parents were always overweight and as such were unable to help me, though they did sympathize. My mother was a constant supply of misinformation, since she had been on every imaginable fad diet. Such diets were obviously not my answer.

I began to gather information. While the kids in my class read about Tom Sawyer's adventures and Superman comics, I searched through diet and nutrition books and articles. But, ironically, it was my first summer job, at the age of fourteen as a Good Humor boy, that proved to be my most practical lesson in weight control.

I quickly learned that to have as much money as possible left at the end of the day, I had to stop eating and drinking up the profits. Instead of orange drinks I turned to water and I learned to eat only one Good Humor Toasted Almond Bar per day. On top of that I was walking -- with two twenty-five-pound ice chests, which contained the tempting ice cream and orange drinks, slung across each shoulder -- along miles of Coney Island Beach. It seemed like a summer spent in the Sahara Desert. But the effect of my combined new-found discipline and daily activity was wonderful weight loss.

When I returned to school in the fall I was a new person. Not only had I saved money, but also I was almost where I should have been on

1

the weight and height charts. Most importantly I was able to look at ice cream and other cherished treats and, if I preferred, walk away from them.

Since then I have studied human nutrition, culinary arts and hotel and restaurant administration. I've learned about cuisines around the world, past and present, and have kept up with the Government's scientific approach that uses such guides as the Recommended Dietary Allowance and the Dietary Goals for the U.S. I have researched more radical approaches to eating, such as macrobiotic cooking and fruitarianism, have read diet philosophies of major religions, and have studied the concepts of a holistic approach to health. I've even made a hobby out of reading "diet" books.

The lessons learned have all aided in the formulation of my philosophy or guide to eating sensibly. I introduced this philosophy to the Maine Chance Beauty Resort where it and my recipes have been put to the test for over a decade. Many women return to Maine Chance yearly. Those who stay slim, who seem to be "naturally" slender, are those who have learned to live by, or have long lived by, the habits and attitudes outlined in this book.

You will find no calorie charts, no daily menus that must be followed, no special foods to eat. *Golden's Kitchen* is written for persons who enjoy cooking and dining, and who also recognize food's significance to their well-being. I hope that after reading this book and trying out some recipes and menus, you will find that combining artistic cooking with a diet philosophy need not conflict. This diet philosophy can be combined with any existing cookbook, whether it be French, Italian or Hungarian, to produce a more colorful, lively, easily digestible cuisine; while giving insight into food's relationship to our well-being so we can sit back, relax and truly experience the pleasures of the palate.

I hope you enjoy this book and find it beneficial.

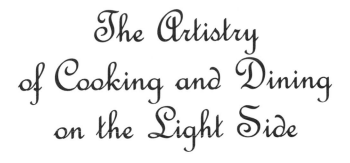

The Artistry
of Cooking and Dining
on the Light Side

Gradually cooking and dining have emerged into a new fare. With few boundaries it is now spontaneous, creative, fresh and simple, old-fashioned as well as new. It is international or all-American. It is eclectic cuisine.

The culinary peacock revolution is here: everything goes provided it is done with good intentions and reasonably good taste. Not only is food preparation and presentation being experimented with, but sets of china and linens are mixed and matched to produce new mood-manipulating heights. Even ancient wine traditions are being toyed with to suit personal preference and to produce exciting food and wine couplings.

The emphasis is decidedly on creativity and enjoyment while entertaining. Hosts and guests have a growing awareness that sharing food intimately connects with our deepest feelings. While eating, all our senses are put to use -- while dining, we communicate, celebrate and share. This combination is truly one of life's given pleasures.

But what of the "few" boundaries mentioned earlier? We can call them a diet philosophy, if philosophizing is your pleasure. Or we can simply call them a guide to help prevent:
1. Obesity
2. Poor health
3. The crazy diet, yo-yo syndrome
4. An ambivalent, love-hate relationship with food

Let's divide this preventative guide into three quick and simple principles -- principles which are not new at all.

PRINCIPLE 1:
Consume a Balanced Variety of Mostly Natural Foods

For millions of years mankind ate of the plants and trees and of living creatures on earth. Then, not too long ago, man invented machines and so began to invent and manipulate his own food.

3

At first man did not foresee a difference. For he still ate mostly the food that nature provided. When man continued to produce more food, he began to eat mostly the food he made or changed, and he realized that too much machine-produced food prevented him from obtaining the soundest of health. Now man under-stands that he, too, is part of nature. He realizes that he, too, must eat mostly the food that nature has provided.

Consume **mostly** natural foods, not necessarily **only** natural foods. Food products made from or processed with high amounts of sugar, fat, salt and chemical preservatives can be eaten in smaller quantities with no harm. All things in nature have levels of tolerance. Bend a branch of a tree a little and there is absolutely no harm done. Bend it back all the way down to the ground and, more than likely, it will snap.

Consume a **balanced variety** of foods. Eating a particular food alone is not enough to be well nourished. No one food or food family supplies all the nutrients needed to maintain good health for most people. (There are always those who are exceptions to the rule.) If we were to eat only fruit, vegetables and rice, our diet would be severely lacking in protein. A diet consisting of only meat, poultry and fish would be void in dietary fiber, Vitamin C and other important nutrients.

Here is a simple and fun rule to follow to obtain a balanced variety of foods that is also tapered to individual need:

THE NINE FINGER RULE

Assuming you are eating three meals a day. For each meal eat an equivalent portion of high protein content foods (fish, meat, poultry, eggs, nuts, cheese, beans) that would be the approximate size of your three largest fingers. All totaled that would be about nine fingers per day. Also, consider every eight-ounce cup of milk or yogurt as two fingers.

Keep in mind that you can eat any number of fingers in one sitting; it doesn't have to be three. For example, you can eat a large Porterhouse steak the size of all nine fingers, but there is no need for more protein during the rest of the day. So if you plan on eating a large meal for dinner, it is wise to skip the bacon and eggs for breakfast.

When you have established your daily allowance of protein, the major portion of your diet should be a variety of complex (naturally occurring) carbohydrates such as fruits and vegetables, whole-grain breads and cereals, brown and wild rice. Eat enough until you feel satisfied. It's that easy!

I think you will find the Nine Finger Rule a good "rule of thumb."

There once was a man named Bogurt,
who decided to eat only yogurt.
He claimed he would stay healthy,
He said he would become trim.
Bogurt, proud of his newly found fruition,
died from malnutrition.

PRINCIPLE 2:
Practice Eating and Drinking in Moderation Through Positive Self-Discipline

> *"In all things not too much," said Socrates, and likewise, Aristotle spoke of the "Golden Mean." What these great philosophers were saying over two thousand years ago, and that holds true today, is that the extreme in any direction is often grounds for suspicion about the quality of our adjustment. If we practice moderation and stay well within the bounds of the extremes, chances are we will stay out of much trouble.*

It is a balance of life's pleasures that leads to fulfillment. No matter how self-satisfied they may temporarily be, food faddists and exercise zealots fail to live the full life that is possible by putting those extreme interests in place with others.

Eating in moderation means eating only when hungry and stopping when satisfied, not stuffed. This is nature's way of counting calories.

The key to moderation is positive self-discipline. This is done by preferring rather than demanding of ourselves. It is also looking at the situation on the positive side.

When we prefer to give something up, it becomes just another daily part of our life. The choice is ours. When we demand ourselves to give something up, we leave no alternative. Leaving no alternative takes away our free will. As a result, consciously or unconsciously we often do just the opposite to regain our independence, somewhat like a child who comes from an over-restrictive home. Also, when we find our self-discipline lacking, we feel unworthy and often guilty. After all, we could not do what we were supposed to do.

This idea literally lets us have our cake and eat it too -- by not eating it all at one sitting. The choice is ours. Through practice, the strain and effort to learn self-control is replaced by the automaticity of habit. It begins to feel easy and natural to do what is best for us.

PRINCIPLE 3:
Keep Physically Active

> *"Eating properly will not by itself keep well a person who does not exercise; for food and exercise, being opposite in effect, work together to produce health."*
>
> — *Hippocrates*

Whether living in trees, caves, castles, igloos or log cabins, for millions of years our ancestors lived a physically active existence. Then around the beginning of the twentieth century technology took away our ancestors' physical chores. With automation and robots, the blue-collar worker is now outnumbered by the white-collar worker for the first time in history. That means a lot of people are sitting for long periods of time which was most unusual to our ancestors.

Here lies the problem. Our bodies have been genetically developed throughout the evolution of man; and they run at peak efficiency based on our ancestors' more physically active existence. We think and sleep better, have greater stamina, strength, endurance, coordination and resistance to illness, and our metabolism and digestive system work best when we are active the way our ancestors were for millions of years. A racing car built to run at speeds over one hundred fifty miles per hour will perform poorly if continually driven at thirty miles per hour. That is the predicament many of us are in now.

The answer: Make physical activity part of your lifestyle like taking a shower and getting dressed in the morning. Have a variety of activities that you prefer doing. Activity is so essential that it should be considered a nutrient. Like a nutrient, the benefits of activity cannot be stored for long. It is best to keep active each day to achieve and maintain physical fitness and good health.

Regular physical activity plus eating a nutritious balanced diet in moderation with a positive mental attitude is the best way to lose weight and keep it off. We needn't count our daily caloric intake nor count our caloric expenditure. (Let the accountants worry about the debits and credits.) If we still feel a need to lose more weight, increase the level of physical activity. Perhaps five to ten more minutes of added daily physical activity will bring us down to the desired weight. But, take heed. Dr. Jean Mayer in his book *A Diet for Living,* claims studies have demonstrated scientifically something which friendly observers had found empirically: ladies want to be thinner (by at least two dress sizes) than men would like them to be. If you are a well-built, healthy, attractive size twelve, please don't try to be a size eight simply because it is the fashion among models -- most often it's not worth the sacrifice.

> *Taking care of the plants and flowers*
> *is the way I spend unsorted hours;*
> *pushing the earth aside, setting a seed below,*
> *stepping back to watch a wonder grow;*
> *bending and stretching hands to the ground,*
> *pruning and trimming, keeping both of us sound.*
> *I think part of life's unsung story*
> *is helping to bestow nature's glory.*

It is important to mention that all three principles deal with habits and attitudes that cannot be bought in a package nor found in a pill. We are ready to change our habits and attitudes **only** when we realize that no one can make that change for us. Nutritionists, doctors and other people in the diet and health profession can only guide and suggest.

So there we have it, the boundaries, the underlying philosophy or guide to *The Artistry of Cooking and Dining on the Light Side.* **Now let's have fun!**

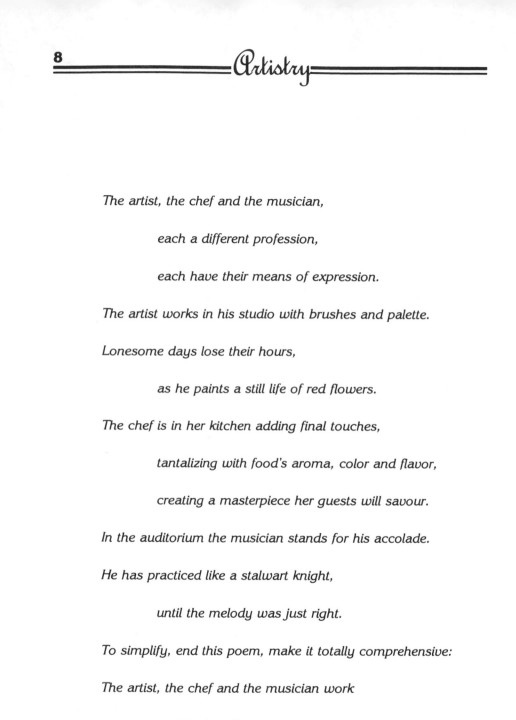

The artist, the chef and the musician,

each a different profession,

each have their means of expression.

The artist works in his studio with brushes and palette.

Lonesome days lose their hours,

as he paints a still life of red flowers.

The chef is in her kitchen adding final touches,

tantalizing with food's aroma, color and flavor,

creating a masterpiece her guests will savour.

In the auditorium the musician stands for his accolade.

He has practiced like a stalwart knight,

until the melody was just right.

To simplify, end this poem, make it totally comprehensive:

The artist, the chef and the musician work

to stimulate the senses.

Artistry

*"Artistic cooking is cooking with the knowledge of
food ingredients and food preparation techniques
to create dishes that have
maximum eye, smell and taste appeal."*

There is much to be said about food preparation techniques; the subject has already filled volumes. Though actual technique is something that can be practiced, improved upon and finally perfected, there are several steps that must first be taken.

These steps may seem obvious but are, in fact, often overlooked. It is imperative, if you want to be not just a good cook but an artistic cook, that you be creative, plan the meal, and purchase the best ingredients. Last but not least, you must work to stay ahead of yourself in the kitchen.

BE CREATIVE

Mrs. Anna Jay was a distinguished hostess for many years at Maine Chance. Like everyone else, she had her likes and dislikes. Her favorite desserts were anything with lemon, fruit and whipped cream. On Saturday night, when we traditionally serve fancy desserts to Maine Chance guests (a test of their self-discipline), I decided to make Mrs. Jay's dream dessert. I baked a cookie crust in a flan mold then filled it with a tart lemon custard. On top of the custard was placed a lemon mousse topped with a pattern of fresh fruit brushed with apricot glaze. The border of the dessert was decorated with whipped cream. Without the realization that the cake was designed for her, Mrs. Jay said casually while eating the dessert, "If I ever get married again, I would like to have this as my wedding cake." Hence, a new Saturday night special dessert was born -- "Mrs. Jay's Wedding Cake."

Work at being creative. Keeping a recipe file is important; it is reassuring to know you can always make the same dish again with the same delicious results. Good cookbooks are a necessity for finding interesting ideas and recipes for the next meal you plan to prepare. But, to enjoy cooking as an art form, learn to be creative by developing your own new dishes. Preparing the same dishes repeatedly is like an artist painting the same picture again and again. Each time you plan a meal, develop one new dish. It can be a salad, dessert or even a drink. The more you practice, the easier recipe development becomes and, of course, the better the new creations taste.

By using your imagination you can correct mistakes in the kitchen and even in the dining room. Some of the best recipes have been "developed" by accident. Had it not been for Henri Charpentier's spontaneous creativity the sweet pancakes that accidently caught fire in a restaurant dining room would have given a meal a disastrous ending. Instead, he dramatized the situation and named the new dessert after a young lady sitting at the table. The new creation -- "Crepes Suzette."

Don't wait until you must save the day to try an idea; if something or someone inspires you -- go for it. One of the greatest French chefs, Auguste Escoffier, invented scores of outstanding dishes. After watching Nellie Melba, the famous Austrian soprano, perform at the opera house, Escoffier was so moved he decided to create a new dish in her name. He placed peaches on vanilla ice cream between the wings of an ice swan covered with spun sugar. He called the dessert "Peach Melba."

Another one of his creations was born when Nellie Melba was on a diet that included a thin slice of toast. Escoffier grilled a piece of toast, split it through the middle and cooked it a second time until it was brown on each side. He called this thin, crunchy creation "Melba Toast."

When developing new dishes, keep the following in mind:

1. **Use a variety of shapes and colors.** Carrots and peas are a simple classic example -- green round peas with diced orange carrots. A cooked vegetable plate consisting of potatoes, sliced turnips and cauliflower will not look nearly as interesting as sliced potatoes, diced beets and broccoli.

2. **Use a variety of textures.** Smooth soft ice cream on top of a crunchy sugar cone has made the ice cream cone one of the most popular all-time treats. Beef Wellington, truly a gourmet dish, has a crunchy pastry crust, a smooth liver paté, and chewy meat (hopefully not too chewy). Try adding some toasted nuts to a light airy souffle or some fresh vegetables into a cottage cheese mixture.

3. **Balance food ingredients.** A person may have some inborn talent for developing interesting taste combinations the way a person is born with an ear for music. But for the most part, knowing how to balance food ingredients so they will appeal to most people's taste buds (you cannot please everyone all the time), comes from plenty of cooking and tasting experience.

There are few foods that will not blend with each other; more important than selecting the right combination is obtaining the proper balance. For example, pickles and ice cream can taste well together providing a small amount of pickle is used just to give the ice cream an interesting nuance.

4. **Season cautiously.** Use herbs and spices sparingly, then taste. More can always be added, but it is difficult to take the taste away once a dish is overseasoned. For the most part, herbs and spices should not mask the flavor of the original ingredients. Instead, they should play a subtle and secondary role. A bowl of chili in which the fiery taste of the chili peppers is so strong that one cannot taste the beans or anything else is far from excellent. Instead, the chili should have a spicy, beefy, tomato flavor. The flavor of the chili beans, when bitten into, can be tasted and even a slight hint of oregano, if added, may be detected.

5. **Garnish and surprise.** One way to make a dish interesting is to garnish using such foods as radish roses, cut vegetables, fresh herbs, black olives, lemon curls and a host of other foods that make the completed dish more attractive. Another way to make dishes interesting is

to surprise your diners. Picture eating a fortune cookie for the first time with no knowledge of the fortune inside. Crepes are interesting because you never know what may be inside. Hide a few nuts in a meat dish. Put a dried apricot or prune on the bottom of a dish of homemade apple- sauce and watch the response.

A final thought about creating new dishes -- if the dish you were de- vising does not come out well and you feel it is a real disaster, a dish you wouldn't want to eat, do not serve it. Put it away and maybe you can do something with it tomorrow or the next day. If there is time left, make an old standby recipe that you know will be successful, or buy a prepared dish at a grocery store or restaurant. There is no such thing as a mistake in the kitchen. It is only a mistake when the food that should not be served is served.

IT STARTS WITH THE MENU

The menu is to the chef as the score is to the musician. There are times when you are alone or with friends and family and no menu is nec- essary. It is fun to improvise and put together whatever is in the kitchen at the moment. However, if you are planning a breakfast, luncheon or dinner party and would like to go about it in the most efficient manner, a menu is necessary.

The menu is most often planned around the main dish or entree. For simple, light dining, the entire meal may consist of just the entree and possibly an accompanying roll and beverage. For example, a chef's salad with a roll and a glass of iced tea can suffice for a simple luncheon. A more elaborate meal may consist of cocktails, hors d'oeuvres, soup, salad, the entrée (which often includes a protein food such as meat with accompanying vegetables), dessert and beverages. The modern trend is going away from elaborate meals with many courses and, instead, keep- ing the menu simple with possibly two or three courses at most. A salad is not necessary when there are plenty of vegetables served. Instead of having soup *and* salad, have soup *or* salad. Even dessert is not always necessary when the meal is accompanied by fresh fruit. A smaller and simpler menu is not only easier for the host or hostess to prepare but is easier on the guests' stomachs and waistlines as well.

Here are some suggestions to keep in mind when planning a menu:

1. **Plan your menu based on the foods that are in season and buy the best ingredients you can find.** If you are planning to serve fish, find out what fish is available at the time and then plan your menu accordingly. Try to use fresh fruits and vegetables that are also in season.

Build a relationship with the butcher, Fishmonger and produce per- son. Let them know your appreciation for good quality. In every batch of meat, fish, eggs and produce there are always the choice specimens. Suppliers will often be glad to save or purchase the best for you if they know your appreciation for it.

Lastly, when making desserts, use real whipping cream, pure vanilla extract, the best chocolate, ice cream and nuts available and don't forget

-- there is no substitute for butter.

2. **Plan your menu with equipment and space in mind.** Don't plan two oven dishes that call for different temperatures at the same time unless you have two ovens. Avoid cooking five things on top of the stove when you have only four burners. Check to see that you have plenty of refrigeration space for storage of cold food items.

3. **Take time to visualize the dishes on the menu as they will appear when served.** The dishes should have a variety of shapes, colors and textures. Try not to serve the same food twice even though the preparation methods vary. There are exceptions to this rule but no menu should contain tomato juice, meat with tomato sauce and lettuce and tomato salad. Variety is the spice of the menu -- in the cooking, in the color of salads and vegetables, and in the garnishes and the flavors.

4. **Vary the temperature of the courses on the menu.** A cold salad, a hot entree and a hot sauce over ice cream makes for an interesting meal.

5. **Give your menu a little of the old and a little of the new.** Food is closely related to the psyche. We feel comfortable eating a dish that we can identify with. A freshly baked bread or corn-on-the-cob gives us a homey welcomed feeling. We have eaten these foods before and have enjoyed them; we are often happy to have them again. On the other hand, most people are adventurous by nature and enjoy exploring. An exotic dish, possibly ethnic or one just created, will lend interest and excitement to the dinner. The dish in itself will become a conversation piece during the meal. If the unusual dish is too diverse for some people, they can find solace with the traditional dish.

The menu is written and the food is purchased. Here are three concepts which I consider very important to keep in mind while preparing the meal.

1. **Keep ahead at all times.** The French chefs call it "mise en place" (pronounced *mee-zon-plass*) and the Chinese chefs are experts at it.

A most important attribute to being a top-notch cook is the ability to have all of the dishes prepared and ready to be served at a chosen time. A person can prepare the most exquisite meal, but if the guests have to wait past bedtime to eat, there's nothing left to rave about.

Before starting to prepare any meal, whether it be a simple breakfast or a four-course dinner, take time to analyze the menu. Find out the items that will take the longest time to cook, what dishes can be prepared ahead of time, what are the last minute chores. It's like playing a game of chess. Every move counts, it's the total amount of correct moves that wins the game.

Before cooking a dish have your utensils out, measure the flour, crack the eggs, cut and trim the vegetables. Bake the cake the day before. Roast the chickens in the morning or afternoon and have them trimmed and waiting to be heated just before serving time. (Be sure to either refrigerate below 45° or hold in the oven at 140° or above to retard bacterial growth.) Leave nothing to be done later because there will

always be something to do at the last second.

The same idea should be applied to the dining room. Have your table set well in advance. Have the serving dishes and utensils out on the kitchen counter ready to be used. Set up the coffee cups, saucers and spoons in the kitchen or in the dining room even though they are not going to be placed on the table until after the meal. Last of all, have the garbage disposal and dishwasher empty so they will be ready for peak periods.

2. **Kin cayw.** For twelve summers I worked as a food director for a children's summer camp. The kitchen staff I worked with were most often young, aspiring cooks or high school and college students. It was easy to teach them cooking skills such as broiling and grilling. We learn quickly the things we enjoy doing, and it's fun to charcoal broil hot dogs, hamburgers and steaks or flip pancakes with a long flexible spatula. The hardest skill to teach them was to clean up after each job before starting the next one, and to make sure serving platters were presented as neatly as possible. These are often-neglected cooking skills that are just as important as being able to charcoal broil steaks to the desired doneness.

To help teach these skills a large sign on the kitchen wall read "Kin Cayw." Only the kitchen personnel knew what these secret words meant and we pledged our allegiance to them. On behalf of all the past camp kitchen crews I have worked with, I would like to divulge the meaning of these secret words.

"Kin" -- keep it neat. Picture the platter or serving dish as the artist's canvas. The most beautiful picture in the world would have little value if it were full of the artist's fingerprints and paint smudge marks. Keep the border of the serving dishes spotless and shining.

"Cayw" -- clean as you work. After each dish is prepared, clear your work area of unneeded utensils and food items. Start your next task with a clean work table. Try using the same utensils over again by quickly rinsing them out or wiping them off. This will prevent undue cluttering of the sink with numerous pots and pans and will make cleanup faster and easier.

3. **Always taste.** All chefs can tell stories of occasions when they did not bother, or forgot, to taste the food. Only later, after the dish had been brought back from the dining room, did they find out that salt had been accidentally used in place of sugar, or a tablespoon of pepper had been used instead of a teaspoonful. A small taste while cooking and before serving is a cook's guarantee of quality.

AND A FINAL WORD

A good meal is not only delicious food well served, it is also dining in a pleasant atmosphere. When we dine, we dine with all our senses. Flowers, soft music in the background, candlelight, comfortable chairs, a table with plenty of room to accommodate the diners, proper room temperature, beautiful and spotlessly clean plates and silverware -- these are all important factors -- factors that will transform artistic cook-

ing into artistic dining.

My wife, Sandy, and I sat outside on a dining room terrace watching fishing boats in the distance slipping in and out of the harbor in Ogunquit, Maine. It was a clear, sunny day with a slight breeze. Birds were flying from tree to tree, and I listened to their chirping sounds. I wondered what they were saying, what form of communication they had with each other. We ordered strawberry daiquiries, a basket of steamed clams and corn-on-the-cob. The daiquiries were fresh tasting, garnished with a bright red strawberry. The clams were juicy and tender. And the corn was sweet and flavorful, the way you expect corn to taste but seldom does. It was a simple meal that pleased all of the senses. That meal is one of my fondest memories.

An Important Word About the Menus and Recipes

Most of the following recipes are used at Maine Chance. They are proven recipes that work, are designed to feed six people and coincide with the diet philosophy using a balanced variety of mostly natural foods. Fruits, vegetables and whole grain foods are used extensively along with ample protein.

Throughout the menus there are a number of rich desserts (designated by the little star) made with plenty of butter, whipped cream, real chocolate, ice cream, honey and sugar. Leaving them out or substituting them for desserts made from artificial sweeteners, carob, dessert toppings and other "low cal" ingredients would miss the essence of the diet philosophy. Simply stated -- enjoy quality, not quantity. However, if you would like to use these menus and recipes to lose weight, I would suggest going very easy on the rich desserts, leaving them out entirely or substituting fresh fruit.

Alcoholic beverages have been left out except as ingredients used in recipes. It is not that I feel these beverages in moderation fail to compliment this cuisine. Instead, viable alternatives have been introduced that may be viewed as a change of pace. By all means, serve cocktails or your favorite wines and beers with these meals if you wish. I do.

The menus appear in a graduated order. That is, from a lighter morning fair to a full course dinner. However, suiting any given occasion, all menus may be interchanged. It's nice to have pancakes or eggs for dinner every once in a while.

Menu
1

Apple-Orange Punch

Baer's Eggs in Casserole
(baked eggs with vegetables, sausage and sherry)

Braided French Bread

Apple-Orange Punch

Ingredients:

1 quart apple juice

1 6-ounce can frozen concentrated orange juice

2¼ cups sparkling water

1 thinly sliced orange

1 thinly sliced lime

Method:

Mix apple juice and orange juice concentrate together until orange juice is melted. Just before serving, add sparkling water and pour into punch bowl over ice cubes. Garnish with orange and lime slices.

Baer's Eggs in Casserole

After all the bad press eggs received during the fifties and sixties, about their being a major cause of high cholesterol, nutritionists now universally agree that eggs are once again okay to eat. Let's face it, even our ancestors while living in trees millions of years ago were busy pilfering eggs from birds' nests to eat. So let's stop worrying about eating eggs and enjoy them. If we need to ponder about something, we can always try to answer the aged question: What came first, the chicken or the egg?

Ingredients:

1½ cups diced onions

1½ cups diced green pepper

1½ cups diced red pepper

1½ cups diced Italian sausage, hot or sweet depending on your preference

3 large tomatoes peeled and diced (peel tomatoes by immersing them in boiling water for 10 minutes)

1 bay leaf

2 tablespoons chopped parsley

2 cups water

6 eggs

½ cup green peas

1 pound cooked broccoli (see About Cooking Vegetables, page 200)

12 strips pimientos

Dry sherry wine

Method:

1. In a large, preferably nonstick, frypan over medium high heat, pla e onions, peppers and sausage. Cook until onions are translucent and there is some browning around the edges. Add tomatoes, bay leaf, parsley and water. Cook mixture, stirring on occasion, until liquid has evaporated.

2. Spread sausage mixture on the bottom of a large ovenproof casserole dish. Crack eggs and gently place them over sausage mixture, taking care not to break the egg yolks. Decorate with green peas, broccoli and pimientos. Sprinkle lightly with sherry.

3. Cover casserole with aluminum foil and bake in a preheated 400-degree oven for about 20 minutes until egg whites have completely cooked through.

Braided French Bread

Ingredients:

1 cup water

1 cup milk

1 tablespoon granulated sugar

1 tablespoon butter

1 tablespoon salt

1 package dry or ⅔ ounce compressed yeast

1 cup gluten flour

3 cups unbleached all-purpose flour

3 cups whole-wheat flour

Cornmeal

Poppyseeds

Method:

1. Heat water and milk to about 100 degrees or the temperature of a warm bath.

2. Combine water, milk, sugar, butter, salt and yeast in a bowl. Let stand a few minutes to give yeast a chance to grow.

3. Add flours to make a dough firm enough to hold its shape, but still slightly sticky. It is advisable to add the last cup of whole-wheat flour slowly until proper consistency.

4. Knead the dough by turning out on a lightly floured worktable. Dust your hands with a little flour. Push your fingers into the dough and then press down with the heels of your hands, rolling the dough back and forth as you press. Keep kneading for about 5 minutes until

the dough is elastic and satiny in texture.

5. Place dough in a lightly oiled bowl and cover with a damp towel or with plastic wrap. Set bowl in a warm place, around 80 to 100 degrees. This can be near a warm stove or on a table in front of a sunny window.

6. When dough is double in bulk, deflate by punching it with your hand a few times.

7. Divide dough into thirds. Roll out each piece so that the center is about 2 inches in diameter tapering gradually at each end. Braid the pieces together and tuck in ends. Place on a sheet pan sprinkled with cornmeal and set in a warm place to rise.

8. Meanwhile, place a pan of water in oven and preheat to 350 degrees.

9. When dough has doubled in bulk, brush lightly with water, sprinkle with poppyseeds and bake for about 50 minutes at 350 degrees. Serve warm with butter.

Menu 2

Cranapple Nedlogs

*(crepes filled with ricotta cheese, dates and pecans,
served with cranapple sauce and fresh fruit)*

Cranapple Nedlogs

I must admit, I burned the cranapple sauce the first time I started to put this dish together. At home with my cranapple sauce, cooking away to reduce it to proper consistency, I sat down for a rest in a comfortable chair. The next thing I knew, I was waking up to the ring of a telephone while the smell of burning cranapple sauce filled the house. Luckily my favorite saucepan was saved by the bell.

I cannot think of any dish that I have had more success with than Cranapple Nedlogs. They are whole-wheat crepes filled with a mixture of ricotta cheese, pecans, dates and a little vanilla extract. Topped with cranberry-applesauce and garnished with fresh fruit, they make a light, healthy meal that appeals to one's sweet tooth. The entire meal is naturally sweetened and, in addition, it has contrasting color, texture, shape and temperature. How can you go wrong?

Whole-Wheat Crepes
(makes 16 crepes)

Ingredients:

3 eggs

1 cup milk

¾ cup whole-wheat flour

Method:

1. Combine all ingredients in a large bowl and beat with a wire whip until a smooth batter is formed. Refrigerate for at least 2 hours or overnight.
2. On a medium high burner, heat a nonstick 8½-inch frypan until it is hot enough so that a drop of water bounces around the pan.
3. Pour a very thin layer of batter in frypan (approximately 1 ounce). Rotate pan to make sure batter covers entire bottom of pan.
4. When the crepe is set (becomes loose from the frypan and begins to show brown edges), turn crepe on other side and cook for about 15 seconds. Set crepes aside.

Ricotta Cheese Filling
(for 12 crepes)

Ingredients:

1 quart ricotta cheese

½ cup chopped pitted dates

(ingredients continued on next page)

½ cup chopped pecans

½ teaspoon pure vanilla extract

Method:

1. Mix all of the ingredients together. Place a 3-ounce portion of cheese mixture on ends of each crepe. Roll crepe. Place each crepe on a lightly greased or nonstick baking pan, making sure there is a small space between each crepe. Set aside.

Cranapple Sauce
(makes about 1 pint)

Ingredients:

6 apples peeled and chopped

1 cup fresh cranberries

1 pint apple juice

Method:

1. In a saucepan, cook apples and cranberries over medium heat until apples are tender and the liquid has been reduced to form a chunky applesauce-like consistency. Refrigerate until slightly chilled.

Garnishes for Plates

Ingredients:

6 beds of Boston, romaine or green leaf lettuce

18 large fresh strawberries washed with caps left on or 6 bunches of grapes

6 ¼-inch slices of orange

6 sprigs of fresh mint (Mint is an easy herb to grow. Try keeping a pot of mint in a sunny location in or next to the kitchen.)

Final Assembly

Warm crepes in a 325-degree oven for about 15 minutes. On luncheon plates, place 3 strawberries and an orange slice that has a radius cut into it enabling you to twist it so that it can stand on two ends forming an orange curl. Garnish with a sprig of mint. Just before serving, place a warm crepe on each plate and top with a ⅓-cup slightly chilled cranapple sauce. Serve while crepes are still warm.

Menu 3

Botanical Fruit

Three Cheese Omelet

High-Fiber Bran Muffins

Botanical Fruit

A bowl or platter of mixed fresh fruit can be as invigorating and aesthetically appealing as walking through a botanical garden on a beautiful spring day. Like a garden of plants and flowers, fruit combinations of colors, patterns, shapes, sizes and fragrances are limitless. Try bordering one fruit around another fruit of contrasting color, such as kiwifruit circling a mound of fresh raspberries. Use contrasting shapes and colors that will dazzle the eye, such as a combination of black grapes, whole strawberries, and pineapple triangles, or a combination of blueberries, diced cantaloupe and sliced red plums.

Summer is no doubt the best time to serve interesting combinations of fresh fruit, because there is an extensive variety in the marketplace. A few canned Bing cherries, prunes, jarred kumquats or frozen peaches will mix well with fresh winter fruit. For a touch of color and aroma add a few sprigs of fresh mint.

For this dish, I will let your imagination be your guide.

Ingredients:

6 to 8 cups of a variety of fresh fruit

Method:

1. Vary size of each fruit by slicing, dicing, balling, leaving whole, or pureeing.
2. Serve fruit in a bowl or platter that will suit your particular fruit combination.

Three Cheese Omelet

The omelet is probably the most popular egg dish because of its versatility. It takes little time to heat a pan, crack a few eggs, and add any number and combination of ingredients to make a good tasting, nutritious dish. Once mastered, omelets are fun to make; beating the eggs, swirling, folding and finally depositing the fluffy creation onto a plate or platter. Voila!

The Three Cheese Omelet has ricotta cheese with chopped chives folded into the center with a melted checkerboard across the top made from Swiss cheese and Cheddar cheese. Served with two rows of shredded spinach, it makes for a tasty and interesting-looking omelet.

Ingredients:

12 eggs at room temperature

2 cups ricotta cheese

1 tablespoon chopped chives

(ingredients continued on next page)

¼ teaspoon onion salt

12 1½-inch squares Swiss cheese, ¼ inch in thickness

12 1½ inch squares Cheddar cheese, ¼ inch in thickness

3 cups shredded spinach

tomato

Method:

1. Preheat broiler.
2. Beat eggs with a whisk until well blended.
3. Mix ricotta cheese, onion salt and chopped chives together.
4. Heat a well-seasoned or nonstick 12-inch omelet pan over high heat. Brush pan lightly with butter. When the butter stops sizzling and before it begins to brown, add the beaten eggs.
5. With a wooden spatula make circular motions around the bottom of the pan. Speed is of the essence for lightness and fluffiness. Spread the eggs evenly throughout the pan and cover any breaks in the surface. Cook until the eggs are mostly firm with the surface being somewhat still liquid.
6. Spread ricotta cheese mixture across the center of the eggs. To turn out omelet, gently raise the handle of the pan and let the omelet slide toward the edge of the pan. Fold the edge nearest the handle over the ricotta cheese with the aid of a spatula. Grasp the handle of the pan, palm side up, and turn pan upside down depositing the omelet into a heated oval platter.
7. Lay out a checkerboard pattern of Swiss and Cheddar cheese across the top of the omelet. Place under a broiler until cheese just begins to melt together. Spread a row of shredded spinach on each side of the omelet.
8. Garnish platter with a tomato rose by cutting a continuous strip of tomato peel with a sharp knife then winding peel up to form a rose.

High-Fiber Bran Muffins
(makes 4½ dozen 1½-ounce muffins)
Make plenty and freeze them.

Ingredients:

5 cups unsifted whole-wheat flour

7½ cups miller's bran (purchased in health food stores and most supermarkets)

2 tablespoons baking powder

1½ teaspoons salt

(ingredients continued on next page)

2 cups raisins

10 eggs

1½ cups honey

1 quart skim milk

⅔ cup safflower oil

1½ teaspoon pure vanilla extract

Method:

1. Preheat oven to 375 degrees.
2. In a bowl mix the flour, bran, baking powder, salt and raisins together.
3. Add remaining ingredients and stir until blended.
4. Using a No. 20 scoop, portion out batter in nonstick or lightly greased muffin tins. Bake in 375-degree oven for 20 to 25 minutes.

Menu
4

Fresh Orange Juice

Amaretto Buttermilk Pancakes

*(garnished with coconut, walnuts and raisins,
served with maple syrup, raspberries and yogurt)*

Fresh Orange Juice

No orange juice can compare to juice that has been freshly squeezed, and it will only taste as good as the oranges it has been squeezed from.

Ingredients:
4 pounds oranges, preferably navel if they are juicy and sweet (no pits to fuss with)

Method:
1. Cut oranges in half, squeeze over juicer, strain out pits.
2. Serve in large pitcher with prechilled juice glasses.

Amaretto Buttermilk Pancakes

Ingredients:
1 cup whole-wheat flour

¾ cup unbleached all purpose flour

½ cup yellow cornmeal

1½ teaspoons baking soda

1 teaspoon salt

2 eggs

2 cups buttermilk

3 tablespoons amaretto liqueur

1 tablespoon melted butter

½ cup shredded unsweetened coconut

½ cup dark raisins

½ cup chopped walnuts or pecans

Confectioners' sugar

Maple syrup

Fresh or frozen strawberries

Plain yogurt

Method:
1. In a bowl mix the flours, cornmeal, baking soda and salt together. Add the eggs, buttermilk, amaretto and melted butter. Continue to mix until a smooth batter is formed.
2. Preheat a nonstick griddle so that it is hot enough to make a drop of water bounce across the surface. Spoon batter onto griddle and cook until cakes are puffy, full of bubbles and edges begin to brown.

Flip over and cook other side.

3. Mix coconut, raisins and nuts together. Place pancakes on heated platter, or on heated individual plates. Garnish top with coconut mixture and sprinkle lightly with confectioners' sugar. Serve with maple syrup, raspberries and yogurt on the side.

Menu
5

Hot Apple Cider with Cinnamon

Spinach, Cheese and Mushroom Frittata

Soy Flour Corn Muffins

Hot Apple Cider with Cinnamon

Ingredients:
2 quarts unfiltered apple juice
6 cinnamon sticks

Method:
1. Heat apple juice and pour into mugs with a cinnamon stick.

Spinach, Cheese and Mushroom Frittata
Frittata *(frit-ta-ta)* — a fancy name for an open-faced omelet

Ingredients:
2 tablespoons olive oil
¼ cup chopped green onion
1 clove minced garlic
½ teaspoon cayenne pepper
2 cups thinly sliced mushrooms
2 heads fresh spinach chopped
8 eggs beaten
½ teaspoon chopped basil
1½ cups grated Jarlsberg cheese

Method:
1. In a large (at least 10 inches and preferably wrought iron) skillet, heat 1 tablespoon oil over medium heat. Add onion, garlic and cayenne pepper. Saute until onion is translucent. Add mushrooms and saute for a minute. Add spinach and stir until wilted. Remove mixture from skillet and keep warm.
2. In the same skillet, heat remaining oil over medium heat. Add spinach mixture to eggs and pour into skillet. Sprinkle top with basil and then grated cheese. Cook slowly until bottom is set then place under the broiler for several minutes until top is lightly browned. Turn out on a hot serving platter or serve directly from skillet.

Soy Flour Corn Muffins

Ingredients:
2½ cups yellow cornmeal
1 cup soy flour

(ingredients continued on next page)

2 teaspoons baking soda

½ cup melted butter or safflower oil

½ cup honey

4 eggs

½ cup buttermilk

1 teaspoon vanilla extract

Method:

1. Preheat oven to 375 degrees.
2. In a bowl, combine the cornmeal, soy flour and baking soda. Mix well with a spoon or wire whip.
3. Add the remaining ingredients. Mix until a smooth batter is formed.
4. Scoop or spoon into nonstick or lightly greased muffin tins. Fill three-fourths full.
5. Bake for approximately 25 minutes at 375 degrees. Serve warm with butter or Honey Butter (see recipe on page 35).

Menu 6

Egg Crepes with Fresh Berries and Yogurt

Toasted Orange Date Bread

Honey Butter

Egg Crepes with Fresh Berries and Yogurt

Ingredients:

10 eggs

1½ tablespoons granulated sugar

1½ teaspoons vanilla extract

2½ cups fresh berries in any combination

6 ounces whipped plain yogurt

6 teaspoons brown sugar

Cinnamon

6 sprigs of mint

Method:

1. In a bowl beat the eggs, granulated sugar and vanilla extract.
2. On a medium high burner, heat a nonstick 8½-inch frypan until it is hot enough so that a drop of water bounces around the pan.
3. Pour a very thin layer of batter in pan (approximately 1 ounce). Rotate pan to make sure batter covers entire bottom.
4. When the crepe is set (becomes loose from the frypan and begins to show brown edges) turn out of pan, fold crepe in half (cooked side on the outside) then fold in half again forming a triangle. Continue this procedure until 18 folded crepes are made. Keep warm in a low oven.
5. Before serving, lay out 3 crepes on 6 individual luncheon plates. Place ½ cup berries in center. Top with 2 tablespoons yogurt, then a teaspoon of brown sugar and a final pinch of cinnamon. Garnish with sprig of mint.

Toasted Orange Date Bread

Ingredients:

3 cups whole-wheat flour

2 teaspoons baking soda

1½ cups orange juice

2 tablespoons grated orange rind

2 eggs

¼ cup melted butter

½ cup chopped dates

Method:

1. Preheat oven to 350 degrees.

2. In a bowl, combine the flour and baking soda. Mix well with a spoon or wire whip.

3. Add the remaining ingredients. Mix until a smooth batter is formed.

4. Bake in a 9-inch lightly greased or nonstick loaf pan for about 45 to 50 minutes at 350 degrees. Unmold when done and let cool.

5. Cut into ½-inch-thick slices, lay out on a sheet pan and bake in a 400 degree oven for about 10 minutes.

Honey Butter

Ingredients:

½ pound butter at room temperature

2 tablespoons honey

2 tablespoons milk

Method:

1. Whip butter, honey and milk together. Scoop or pipe mixture through a pastry bag and star tube (see Working with a Pastry Bag, page 204) into small crockery dishes or into paper hors d'oeuvre cups.

Menu
7

Iced Herbal Mint Tea

"Light and Lively"

*(bowl of fresh fruit and yogurt
served with whole-wheat turtle rolls)*

★ **Hot Bourbon Walnut Pie
with Whipped Cream**

Iced Herbal Mint Tea

Ingredients:

8 bags of herbal mint tea

3 quarts water

6 sprigs of fresh mint

6 thin slices of lemon with a radius cut into each

Method:

1. Add tea bags to water and refrigerate for at least 2 hours. Stir, remove tea bags and serve in tall glasses over ice garnished with a sprig of mint and a slice of lemon attached to the rim of the glass.

Bowl of Fresh Fruit and Yogurt

Legend has it that, over two thousand years ago, a nomad traveling across the desert filled his goatskin bag with some milk, slung it across the back of his camel, and traveled on. When he opened the bag hours later, he found his liquid refreshment transformed into a thick, tangy custard.

Since his discovery, yogurt has been glorified as the elixir for good health and longevity. Actually, mankind has always searched in vain for the fountain, the food, the herb, and recently the pill that will cure his ailments.

Yogurt in its unadultered form is good for us, but only a well-balanced diet of other healthy foods will ensure us proper nutrition.

Proper nutrition is good for us, but only a harmonious balance of other good living habits will provide us with good health and longevity.

Ingredients:

1 pint strawberries washed and stemmed

1 small pineapple cut into cubes

1 pint washed black grapes removed from stems or 1 pint washed blueberries

1 small honeydew melon cut into cubes

2 oranges peeled and sectioned

3 cups plain yogurt

¼ cup honey mixed with ¼ cup orange or apple juice

Method:

1. Portion out an even mixture of fruit into 6 individual serving bowls.

Scoop ½ cup yogurt over fruit in center of bowl. Serve with heated orange or apple honey on the side.

Whole-Wheat Turtle Rolls

There is something about eating a roll that has been shaped into an animal that brings out the child in every one of us. Make some rolls into the shapes of alligators, rabbits, turtles and snakes. Cover them up with a napkin in a basket and watch the results: "Look at this; it's a turtle." "And this one is a rabbit." Chuckle ... giggle ... "I can't believe it." "I'm going to save mine." Stimulating and pleasing the senses is what good cooking is all about.

Ingredients:

2 cups milk

1 package dry or ⅔ ounce compressed yeast

1 egg

2 tablespoons butter

¼ cup honey

1 teaspoon salt

½ cup cornmeal

5½ cups unsifted whole-wheat flour

Raisins

1 beaten egg

Method:

1. Heat milk to about 100 degrees or the temperature of a warm bath.
2. Combine milk, yeast, egg, butter, honey, salt and cornmeal in a bowl. Let stand a few minutes to give yeast a chance to grow.
3. Add flour to make a soft and slightly sticky dough. The amount of flour to be added can vary depending on the flour's ability to absorb liquid. It is advisable to add the last cup of flour slowly until a soft and slightly sticky dough is obtained.
4. Knead dough by turning out onto a lightly floured worktable. Dust your hands with a little flour. Push your fingers into the dough and then press down with the heels of your hands, rolling the dough back and forth as you press. Keep kneading for about 5 minutes until the dough is elastic and satiny in texture.
5. Place dough in a lightly oiled bowl to prevent sticking and cover with a damp towel or plastic wrap. Set bowl aside in a warm place around 80 to 100 degrees. This can be near a warm stove or on a table in front of a sunny window.

6. When dough is double in bulk, deflate by punching it with your hand a few times.

7. Assemble turtles as in diagram using raisins for the eyes. Score the backs of the turtles with a sharp knife and pinch out tails. Let turtles rise in a warm place until double in bulk. This should take approximately 20 to 30 minutes.

8. Brush each turtle gently with beaten egg. Bake in a preheated 375-degree oven for approximately 25 minutes until turtles are golden brown.

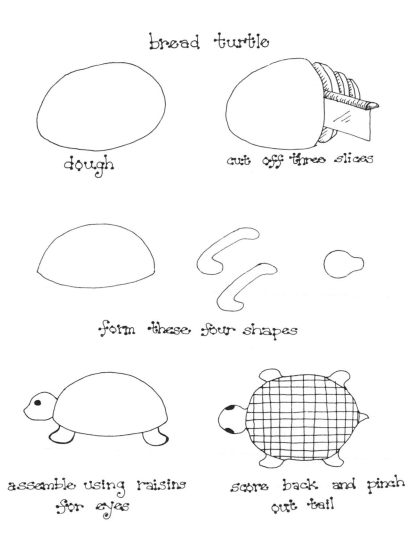

bread turtle

dough   cut off three slices

form these four shapes

assemble using raisins for eyes   score back and pinch out tail

★ Hot Bourbon Walnut Pie with Whipped Cream

Ingredients for pie crust:

⅔ cup unbleached all-purpose flour

⅓ cup whole-wheat flour

¼ pound unsalted butter

¼ cup cold water with ¼ teaspoon dissolved salt

Method:

1. In a large bowl, mix both flours together. Working quickly with your fingertips rub butter into flour until the size of walnuts. Make a well in the center of the flour mix and add just enough water until the dough is held together. (Overmixing and too much water will make a tough pastry.) Turn out dough on table, form into a frisbee shape, cover with plastic wrap and refrigerate for at least 1 hour.

2. Preheat oven to 400 degrees.

3. Using two 9-inch pie pans, lightly grease the inside of one pan and the outside of the other. Roll out pastry on a lightly floured table into a circle ¼ inch thick. Roll pastry over rolling pin to help transfer into the pie pan that has the inside greased. Trim pastry and cover with pie pan that has been greased on the ouside. Bake in 400-degree oven for 20 to 30 minutes until crust is a light golden brown. (This process, called baking the pie crust "au blonde" before adding any filling, helps to produce pies that do not have soggy, uncooked bottom crusts.) Let cool before adding filling.

Ingredients for filling:

3 eggs at room temperature

1 cup brown sugar

1 cup light Karo corn syrup heated to about 160 degrees

2 tablespoons melted unsalted butter

1 tablespoon bourbon

1 teaspoon vanilla extract

¼ teaspoon salt

2½ cups shelled walnuts

Method:

1. Preheat oven to 350 degrees.

2. Beat eggs lightly. Mix in remaining ingredients. Pour into prepared pie shell and bake in 350-degree oven for approximately 35 to 40 minutes. When done, filling should be slightly less set in center than around edge. To serve warm, pie can be kept in a 175-degree oven.

Heating in a microwave oven will tend to make the crust and top of pie less crunchy.

Ingredients for whipped cream:

1 cup well-chilled heavy cream
3 tablespoons brown sugar
½ teaspoon vanilla extract

Method:

1. Add all three ingredients into a well-chilled bowl and beat until soft peaks are formed. Serve on the side in a well-chilled serving bowl.

Menu
8

Boston Lettuce Leaf Salad

Crabmeat or Lobster Lahvosh

Lemon and Lime Oranges

Boston Lettuce Leaf Salad

Ingredients:

3 small or 2 large heads Boston lettuce

½ teaspoon anise seed

French Dressing (see recipe on page 64)

½ cup thinly sliced radishes

¼ cup thinly sliced pitted black olives

Method:

1. Prepare salad greens. (see About Preparing Salad Greens, page 202)
2. Add ½ teaspoon anise seed to French dressing and refrigerate at least 2 hours.
3. Just before serving, toss greens with dressing, radishes and olives, reserving some radishes and olives to garnish top of salad.

Lobster or Crabmeat Lahvosh

Ingredients:

6 5-inch lahvosh wheat cracker breads (found in most supermarkets)

1½ pounds cooked lobster or crabmeat

1½ cups freshly cooked or canned baby artichokes cut into bite-size pieces

1½ cups fresh mushrooms thinly sliced and blanched (cooked quickly in boiling water until softened)

2 medium tomatoes diced

½ cup cut green onions blanched

6 slices of Dofino or Muenster cheese, ¼ inch in thickness

Method:

1. Preheat oven to 400 degrees.
2. Lay out lahvosh crackers on a sheet pan. Portion ingredients out evenly on each cracker in the order of the ingredients.
3. Just before serving, bake in 400-degree oven for 10 to 15 minutes until cheese is completely melted.

Lemon and Lime Oranges

Ingredients:

7 large navel oranges

1 lemon

1 lime

3 tablespoons brown sugar

6 strawberries and/or 6 sprigs of mint

Method:

1. Using a potato peeler, remove the peel from 1 orange, the lemon and the lime, making sure there is no white portion of the membrane left on the peel. Cut peel into very thin 1-inch strips.

2. In a saucepan, add the juice of the orange, the lemon, and the lime. Add brown sugar and peel strips. Cook over high heat for a couple of minutes until the liquid is a syrupy consistency.

3. Cut away the entire peel from the remaining 6 oranges. Cut oranges into round slices. Lay out slices on a serving platter and garnish top with cooked peel and syrup. Garnish top with strawberries or mint sprigs or both.

Menu 9

**Chilled Hibiscus Tea
with Melon, Plums and Lime Slices**

Ensalada Mexicano

*(Mexican-style salad with cheese, chile, guacamole
yogurt, tortilla chips and black olives)*

★ **Papaya Cake with Lemon Butter Frosting**

Chilled Hibiscus Tea
with Melon, Plums and Lime Slices

Ingredients:

6 hibiscus tea bags

2 quarts water

1 cantaloupe melon sliced into wedges

1 small can of plums with juice

1 lime cut into thin slices

Method:

1. Add tea bags to water and let steep for about a half an hour. Stir, remove tea bags, add remaining ingredients and refrigerate for at least 3 hours.

2. Serve well-chilled in a pitcher or punch bowl.

Ensalada Mexicano.

Ingredients:

¾ pound lean ground beef

1½ cups canned western style spiced beans

1 tablespoon chili powder

2 well-ripened (soft to the touch) avocados

2 tablespoons lemon juice

Pinch cayenne pepper

18 cups shredded lettuce (try using a combination of two or more greens)

1 ounce grated Cheddar cheese

2 tomatoes cut into small dice

6 pitted black olives cut into thin slices

½ cup yogurt

½ cup sliced green onion tops

18 tortilla chips

Method:

1. Brown ground beef in skillet, then drain in a colander to remove fat. Place meat back in skillet, add beans and chili powder. Keep warm until serving.

2. Prepare guacamole mixture by mashing the avocado pulp with a fork. Mix in lemon juice and cayenne pepper. Set aside.

3. Portion out 3 cups of shredded lettuce into six 1-quart capacity salad bowls. Sprinkle each bowl with grated cheese, diced tomatoes and black olives.

4. Place a large scoop of chili mixture in center of bowl, top with guacamole, then yogurt, then a sprinkling of green onions. Place 3 tortilla chips around the chili mound and serve.

★ Papaya Cake with Lemon Butter Frosting
(Makes one 9-inch cake)

Ingredients:

¼ pound unsalted butter at room temperature

1¼ cups brown sugar

2 eggs

¼ cup sour cream mixed with 1 teaspoon baking soda

1 cup mashed papaya pulp

1 teaspoon vanilla extract

1⅔ cup unbleached flour

1 teaspoon salt

Method:

1. Preheat oven to 350 degrees.

2. In a mixing bowl, cream butter and sugar. Add eggs gradually and continue beating. Add sour cream mixture and when incorporated add papaya and vanilla extract.

3. Sift the flour and salt together. Add to mixing bowl, beating just until a uniform batter is obtained.

4. Distribute batter into a 9-inch lightly greased or nonstick cake pan. Bake at 350 degrees for about 60 minutes.

5. When cake is cool, cut one-fourth of the top portion of the cake off. Chop top portion into crumbs and toast in a 400-degree oven for about 10 minutes until lightly browned. Ice the remaining cake with Lemon Butter Frosting and sprinkle top with toasted cake crumbs.

Lemon Butter Frosting

Ingredients:

2 tablespoons melted butter

1 cup confectioners' sugar

(ingredients continued on next page)

1 tablespoon milk

1 teaspoon grated lemon rind

1 tablespoon lemon juice

Method:

1. Mix all of the ingredients together.

Menu 10

Diplomat Salad

(cottage cheese, pineapple and watermelon served on beds of Boston lettuce)

Spinach Soufflé

Cornmeal Rye Melba Toast

★ Old-Fashioned Brownies with Homemade Vanilla Bean Ice Cream

Diplomat Salad

Ingredients:

Boston, romaine or green leaf lettuce leaves

1 quart cottage cheese

½ cup drained canned crushed pineapple

6 watermelon wedges, about 2½ inches long and 1½ inches wide

6 pineapple wedges, about 2½ inches long and 1½ inches wide

Method:

1. Line an oval or round platter with lettuce leaves, making sure that the outer parts of the leaves are along the border of the platter and the stalks facing the center.
2. Mix cottage cheese and crushed pineapple together. Mound the cheese mixture in the center of the platter.
3. Arrange watermelon and pineapple wedges alternately around the outside of the platter.

Spinach Soufflé

Ingredients:

Softened butter

Whole-wheat bread crumbs

2½ tablespoons butter

2 tablespoons minced shallots or green onions

1½ cups milk

4½ tablespoons whole-wheat flour

2 heads spinach, cleaned and chopped

¼ cup toasted slivered almonds (toast almonds in 400-degree oven for 12 minutes)

½ teaspoon salt

¼ teaspoon black pepper

¼ teaspoon nutmeg

5 egg yolks

8 egg whites

¼ teaspoon cream of tartar

Method:

1. Preheat oven to 350 degrees.

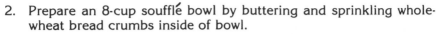

2. Prepare an 8-cup soufflé bowl by buttering and sprinkling whole-wheat bread crumbs inside of bowl.
3. Sauté the minced shallots or onions in butter until soft. Add 1 cup of milk and heat until simmering.
4. Meanwhile, mix together the remaining ½ cup milk and whole-wheat flour. Make a smooth paste and add to simmering milk. Cook, stirring constantly, until mixture comes to a boil and thickens. Remove from heat.
5. In a large kettle of boiling water, blanch the spinach for 1 minute, then drain well by pressing down on spinach with your hands in a colander. Add spinach, almonds, salt, pepper and nutmeg to milk mixture. Add egg yolks one at a time.
6. In a mixing bowl, beat the egg whites until foamy. Add cream of tartar and continue beating until egg whites are stiff and hold their shape, but still have a velvety appearance.
7. Fold egg whites into spinach mixture. Pour mixture into prepared soufflé bowl and sprinkle top with whole-wheat bread crumbs. Place bowl in a pan of water and bake at 350 degrees for 1 hour and 15 minutes.

Cornmeal Rye Melba Toast

Ingredients:

Cornmeal Rye Rolls (see recipe on page 68))

Method:

1. Preheat oven to 350 degrees.
2. Cut rolls into very thin slices, around 1/8 inch in thickness. Lay out on a baking sheet pan. Bake in 350-degree oven for 15 to 20 minutes until crisp. Serve toast in a napkin inside a basket.

Old-Fashioned Brownies
(makes 2 dozen)

Ingredients:

4 ounces unsweetened chocolate

¼ pound unsalted butter

1 cup whole-wheat flour

1 teaspoon baking powder

½ teaspoon salt

3 eggs

1½ cups light brown sugar

1½ teaspoons vanilla extract

1 cup chopped walnuts

1 cup raisins (optional)

Method:

1. Preheat oven to 350 degrees.
2. In a saucepan melt chocolate and butter over very low heat, or in top of a double boiler. Meanwhile, mix the flour with baking powder and salt.
3. Beat eggs in mixing bowl. Add sugar and vanilla; beat well. Blend in chocolate mixture. Add flour mixture, nuts and raisins.
4. Spread batter in a well-buttered 9 by 12 by 1-inch sheet pan. Bake at 350 degrees about 20 minutes until edges shrink slightly from sides of pan. Cool thoroughly; then cut into squares.

Vanilla Bean Ice Cream

Ingredients:

1 cup milk

1 vanilla bean stick

2 eggs

1 cup granulated sugar

¼ cup brown sugar

¼ teaspoon salt

2 cups heavy cream

3 cups milk

Method:

1. In a saucepan bring 1 cup of milk with vanilla bean stick to a simmer. Remove from heat and set aside. Meanwhile, in a mixing bowl beat eggs until foamy, add sugar gradually and continue to beat until stiff peaks are formed.
2. Run your thumb and index finger down the vanilla bean stick and squeeze out beans into mixing bowl. Add remaining ingredients including cup of simmered milk.
3. Freeze in ice cream maker packed with 3 to 4 parts of ice to 1 part of rock salt.

Menu
11

Orange and Almond Salad

Eight Seasons Shrimp or Chicken Salad

Tomatoes, Cucumbers, Purple Onions
and Fresh Dill Weed

Pita Bread

★ Lemon Custard Tarts with Strawberries,
Blueberries and Sliced Peaches

This menu is good for a simple informal buffet luncheon. Let guests make their own shrimp or chicken pocket bread sandwiches, garnishing them with the tomatoes, cucumbers, onions and dill weed. The Orange and Almond Salad accompanies the sandwiches, and please don't let the long recipe for the Lemon Custard Tarts discourage you. The tart shells and the lemon custard can be prepared days in advance. When put together and served, they make one of those desserts that will not be quickly forgotten.

Orange and Almond Salad

Ingredients for Orange Dressing:

2 tablespoons safflower oil

¼ cup tarragon vinegar

½ cup orange juice

1 tablespoon fresh chopped parsley

1/8 teaspoon black pepper

1/8 teaspoon salt

Pinch dry mustard

Honey (add if necessary depending on sweetness of orange juice)

Ingredients for Salad:

12 cups mixed greens (see About Preparing Salad Greens, page 202)

1½ cups orange segments (peel orange and cut out segments with paring knife between membranes)

½ cup slivered toasted almonds (toast almonds in 400-degree oven for 10 minutes)

Method:

1. Make Orange Dressing by mixing all of the ingredients together. Taste for seasoning. Chill dressing well.

2. Before serving, gently toss greens, orange segments and almonds with chilled prepared dressing. Reserve some orange segments and almonds for garnishing the top of the salad. Serve in well-chilled bowl.

Eight Seasons Shrimp or Chicken Salad

Ingredients:

4 cups diced cooked shrimp or chicken

(ingredients continued on next page)

⅔ cup yogurt (for richer mixture use ⅓ cup yogurt and ⅓ cup
    mayonnaise)
2 stalks diced celery
2 carrots peeled and grated
2 hard-boiled eggs chopped
2 tablespoons Eight Seasons Salt (see next recipe)

Method:
1. In a bowl mix all of the ingredients together.

Eight Seasons Salt
(makes 1½ cups)

Use this low-sodium salt as an extra condiment to accompany your
table salt and pepper.

Ingredients:
½ cup dried parsley flakes
2 tablespoons rosehips (for easy availability remove from rosehips
    tea bags)
2 tablespoons dried basil flakes
2 tablespoons garlic salt
1 tablespoon paprika
1 tablespoon grated lemon rind
1 teaspoon cayenne pepper
1 teaspoon crushed saffron

Method:
1. Mix ingredients together, store in container or jar with a tight fitting
    cover.

Pita Bread
(makes 12 pocket breads)

For ease, purchase the store-bought whole-wheat pita bread or use
this recipe to make your own. I must warn you: After making your own,
you may never want to purchase the store-bought variety again.

Ingredients:
1 tablespoon dry yeast
1 tablespoon honey

(ingredients continued on next page)

1 tablespoon oil

1 teaspoon salt

1¼ cups tepid water

3 to 3½ cups whole-wheat flour

Method:

1. Mix yeast, honey, oil, salt and water together. Let stand for about 15 minutes until yeast begins to foam. Add enough flour until a sticky dough is formed.

2. Knead dough by turning out onto a lightly floured worktable. Dust your hands with a little flour. Push your fingers into the dough and then press down with the heels of your hands, rolling the dough back and forth as you press. Keep kneading for about 5 minutes until the dough is elastic and satiny in texture.

3. Place dough in a lightly oiled bowl and cover with a damp towel or plastic wrap. Set bowl aside in a warm place around 80 to 100 degrees. This can be near a warm stove or on a table in front of a sunny window. Let rise until dough is double in bulk.

4. Preheat oven to 425 degrees.

5. Punch dough down and divide into 12 equal pieces. Cover pieces with plastic wrap or a damp towel to prevent them from drying out.

6. On a floured surface roll out balls until they are ¼-inch thick and 4 to 4½ inches in diameter. Place rolled out pieces on a nonstick or lightly oiled baking sheet; keep pieces covered with a damp towel or plastic wrap until ready to bake.

7. Bake in 425 degree oven for 8 to 10 minutes until pockets have puffed up and begin to brown.

Tomatoes, Cucumbers, Purple Onions and Dill Weed

Ingredients:

2 tomatoes

1 cucumber scored

1 purple onion

Bunch of fresh dill weed

Method:

1. Cut tomatoes, cucumber and onion in ¼-inch-thick round slices; lay out alternating and overlapping slices on a serving platter. Trim dill weed into 3-inch-long sprigs and use to garnish serving platter.

★ Lemon Custard Tarts with Strawberries, Blueberries and Sliced Peaches

Ingredients:

¼ pound butter

¼ cup granulated sugar

1 egg

1 teaspoon vanilla extract

1½ cups unbleached all-purpose flour

Method:

1. In a bowl cream butter and sugar. Add egg and vanilla extract. Work in the flour until mixture is blended, adding a little cold water if necessary to make a light dough. Wrap dough in plastic wrap and refrigerate for at least an hour.

2. Roll out dough ¼ inch thick. Cut rounds of dough to line 3-inch tart shells or the backs of muffin tins. Fit the dough into the shells and prick it well with a fork.

3. Bake in preheated 375-degree oven for 15 to 20 minutes until golden brown.

Ingredients for lemon custard:

¼ cup cornstarch

¾ cup and 2 tablespoons granulated sugar

½ cup egg yolks

1 cup milk

¼ cup and 2 tablespoons lemon juice

2 teaspoons grated lemon rind

2 tablespoons unsalted butter

Method:

1. In a bowl mix the cornstarch, sugar, egg yolks until lump-free and thoroughly blended.

2. In a saucepan bring the milk, lemon juice and lemon rind to a boil.

3. Temper egg yolk mixture by adding about one-third of the hot milk mixture into the bowl. Now pour the egg mixture into the saucepan, keep stirring until mixture comes to a boil. Remove from heat, add butter and store in covered bowl in refrigerator until ready to serve.

Ingredients for final assembly of custard tarts:

Lemon custard

6 tart shells

1 cup heavy cream, 3 tablespoons light brown sugar and 1 teaspoon
vanilla extract whipped to soft peaks in a chilled bowl

1 cup strawberries, preferably fresh or frozen

1 cup blueberries, preferably fresh or frozen

1 cup sliced peaches, preferably fresh or frozen

Granola or toasted coconut

Method:

1. Mix in ¼ cup whipped cream into lemon custard to lighten mixture.
    Place a scoop of custard in each tart shell. Spoon a nice dollop of
    whipped cream on top of custard. Surround each tart shell with an
    evenly divided mixture of fruit. Sprinkle toasted coconut on top of
    whipped cream for the final touch!

Menu 12

Tomato Juice Cocktail

**Veal and Vegetable Decoupage
over Spinach Angel's Hair Pasta**

Raspberry Ice with Fresh Strawberries

Tomato Juice Cocktail

Ingredients:

24 ounces tomato juice

1 large tomato peeled and seeded (peel tomato by cutting out core and plunging into boiling water for 10 seconds)

¼ teaspoon Tabasco sauce

6 lime slices

Method:

1. Puree tomato juice, tomato and Tabasco sauce in a blender and chill well. Serve in chilled cocktail glasses with a squeezed slice of lime.

Veal and Vegetable Decoupage over Spinach Angel's Hair Pasta

Take a classic dish that appeals to just about everyone, jazz it up a bit by changing and adding a few ingredients, give it a fancy name and you should have a sure winner that is new and unusual. But you can't fool everyone -- to the average kid it's still meatballs and spaghetti with yucchy vegetables.

Ingredients:

1 quart strong-flavored veal or chicken stock (see Stocks -- Les Fonds de Cuisine, page 197)

¾ pound peeled baby carrots

¾ pound unpeeled baby zucchini or regular zucchini cut into finger-size pieces

¾ pound rutabagas, peeled and cut into 1-inch cubes

1 pint peeled pearl onions

2½ tablespoons Eight Seasons Salt (see recipe on page 55)

3 slices of whole-wheat bread

1½ pounds lean ground veal

¾ pound cooked spinach angel's hair pasta (very thin pasta)

Salt and cayenne pepper to taste

Fresh basil or spinach leaves

Method:

1. Simmer vegetables one at a time in veal stock until tender. Set aside.
2. In a bowl, pour ¾ cup veal stock over the seasoning salt. Let stand

for a couple of minutes. Add bread and mix until a thick paste is formed. Add veal and mix well. Roll mixture into 2-inch diameter balls. Place on a nonstick or lightly greased baking pan. Bake in a preheated 400-degree oven for about 15 minutes until the centers of the veal balls still have a slight trace of pinkness.

3. Place cooked pasta on a large serving platter or dinner plates. Arrange cooked vegetables and veal balls over the pasta. Season the veal stock with salt and cayenne pepper to taste, pour some over the platter and serve the remaining broth in a sauce boat. Garnish platter with fresh basil and spinach leaves and serve.

Raspberry Ice with Fresh Strawberries

Ingredients:

3 pints fresh raspberries

Honey to taste

6 tablespoons yogurt

6 large unstemmed strawberries

Method:

1. Purée raspberries in blender or food processor and strain out seeds through a sieve. Add honey if necessary for extra sweetness. Much will depend on the natural sweetness of the raspberries.

2. Freeze in ice cream maker packed with 3 to 4 parts of ice to 1 part of rock salt.

3. Scoop into 6 chilled dessert dishes. Spoon a dollop of yogurt on top and garnish with a strawberry.

Menu
13

Pineapple Coconut Juice

Earth Salad
*(mixed greens, artichokes, cauliflower, red cabbage,
sprouts and shredded cheese)*

French Dressing

Buttermilk Apple Carrot Muffins

Pineapple Coconut Juice

Ingredients:

1 quart Hansen's Pineapple Coconut Juice

Shaved ice

6 large strawberries

Method:

1. Pour juice over shaved ice in 6 stemmed cocktail glasses. Garnish with strawberries and serve.

Earth Salad

The Earth Salad is served in individual 1-quart capacity salad bowls. Because of the way the cheese is grated the salad gives an earthy bountiful appearance.

Ingredients:

18 cups mixed salad greens (see About Preparing Salad Greens, page 202)

18 small canned or jarred artichoke hearts

1½ cups finely sliced red cabbage

18 bite-size pieces of cauliflower

18 cherry tomatoes

12 ounces finely grated Jarlsberg cheese (Rotary cheese graters can be purchased at most gourmet and restaurant supply stores. The finest grating attachment is used for this salad.)

1 pint radish sprouts or alfalfa sprouts

rotary grater

Method:

1. Place 3 cups of salad greens with 3 artichoke hearts in 6 individual 1-quart capacity salad bowls. Sprinkle with red cabbage. Place 3 pieces of cauliflower, 3 cherry tomatoes and 3 bouquets of sprouts around the sides and the grated cheese in the center.

French Dressing
(makes 1½ cups)

Quite simply, oil is the culprit that adds refined excessive calories to conventional salad dressings. Whether it is in an emulsion, such as mayonnaise, or just mixed with vinegar, most salad dressings have too much oil fit for human consumption.

To lower the calories, other ingredients such as consomme, fruit juice or wine may be substituted for most of the oil. These ingredients add flavor and nutrients while there still is a sufficient amount of oil left in the dressing to give a smooth palatable texture to the salad greens.

Most conventional French dressings are made from 3 parts of oil to 1 part of vinegar. By substituting 2 parts of the oil with chicken stock or consomme, the new dressing has approximately 32 calories as opposed to conventional French dressings having 92 calories per tablespoonful. Best of all, people who have compared the difference between the two dressings usually agree that the new dressing has a lighter, more flavorful taste.

Ingredients:

1 cup chicken consomme or strong-flavored chicken stock
　　(see Stocks -- Les Fonds de Cuisine, page 197)

½ cup red wine vinegar

½ cup safflower oil

2 cloves minced garlic

2 tablespoons chopped parsley

1 teaspoon sugar

Pinch of dry mustard

½ teaspoon pepper

½ teaspoon salt

Method:

1. Mix all of the ingredients together. Chill well before serving.

Buttermilk Apple Carrot Muffins
(makes 16 muffins)

Ingredients:

2½ cups whole-wheat flour

¾ teaspoon baking powder

½ tablespoon baking soda

½ teaspoon salt

½ teaspoon allspice

½ teaspoon nutmeg

1 teaspoon cinnamon

½ cup buttermilk

½ cup honey

½ cup safflower oil

4 eggs

1 teaspoon pure vanilla extract

1½ cups chopped peeled apples

1½ cups grated peeled carrots

Method:

1. Preheat oven to 375 degrees.
2. In a bowl, combine the flour, baking powder, baking soda, salt, allspice, nutmeg and cinnamon. Mix well with a spoon or wire whip.
3. Add the buttermilk, honey, oil, eggs and vanilla. Stir ingredients until blended. Fold in the apples and carrots.
4. Scoop or spoon into nonstick or lightly greased muffin tins, fill three-quarters full.
5. Bake for approximately 25 minutes at 375 degrees. Serve warm with butter.

Menu
14

Asparagus Purée Soup

Cornmeal Rye Rolls with Cheese Spread
and Fresh Fruit

★ Traditional French Macaroons

Asparagus Purée Soup

     Let's for a moment take a look at the ingredients and process that goes into making a traditional creamed soup. A cream of asparagus soup is initially thickened with a roux (pronounced roo) which is a mixture of fat and white flour. After the asparagus has been cooked, the ingredients are passed through a food mill whereby discarding the fibrous portion of the vegetable. A liaison is added to the soup which is a mixture of heavy cream and egg yolks. Then right before serving, in goes a good chunk of softened butter to give the soup a glistening grand finale. It may look good. It may taste good. But how healthy is it? The answer is twofold -- not so bad, if it is once in a while; not healthy at all, if one enjoys a steady diet of creamed soups and other foods rich in fat content.

     The recipe for Asparagus Purée Soup is tasty, easy to prepare and can certainly be part of a person's diet mainstay. The vegetable's fiber serves as a natural thickening agent. Other vegetables may be substituted for asparagus, making any number of thickened soups. My favorite is puree of fresh pea soup, to which I like to add a touch of fresh mint or marjoram.

Ingredients:

¼ chopped green onion

1 tablespoon butter

2 pounds fresh or frozen asparagus

2 cups whole milk or 2% milk

2 cups strong-tasting chicken stock or canned chicken consomme
    (see Stocks -- Les Fonds de Cuisine, page 197)

Salt and white pepper to taste

Fresh cut or frozen chives

Paprika

Method:

1.   In a large pot sauté the onion in butter until translucent.

2.   Add milk, stock and asparagus. Cook uncovered until asparagus is just tender. Avoid overcooking the asparagus in order to maintain a bright green color and a fresh taste.

3.   Purée the ingredients in a blender. Add more milk or chicken stock depending on flavor and thickness desired.

4.   Season to taste with salt and pepper. Garnish with chopped chives and a dash of paprika.

Cornmeal Rye Rolls
(makes about 2 dozen rolls)

Ingredients:

2 cups tepid water

1 tablespoon yeast

2 tablespoons vegetable oil

1 tablespoon salt

1/3 cup honey

2 tablespoons caraway seeds

1/2 cup cornmeal

1 cup rye flour

1 cup gluten flour (found in health food stores and many supermarkets)

3 to 4 cups whole-wheat flour

Method:

1. Combine water, yeast, oil, salt, honey and caraway seeds. Let stand a few minutes to give yeast a chance to grow.

2. Add cornmeal, rye flour, and gluten flour. Add whole-wheat flour until a soft slightly sticky dough is formed.

3. Knead the dough by turning out onto a lighty floured worktable. Dust your hands with a little flour. Push your fingers into the dough and then press down with the heels of your hands, rolling the dough back and forth as you press. Keep kneading for about 5 minutes until the dough is elastic and satiny in texture.

4. Place dough in a lightly oiled bowl, cover with a damp towel or plastic wrap. Set bowl aside in a warm place around 80 to 100 degrees. This can be near a warm stove or on a table in front of a sunny window.

5. When dough is double in bulk, deflate by punching it with your hand a few times.

6. Roll out and divide dough into 2-ounce rolls. Place rolls on a lightly greased or nonstick baking pan. Let rolls rise in warm area until double in bulk. Brush each roll gently with beaten egg. Bake in preheated 375-degree oven for approximately 25 minutes.

Cheese Spread
(makes 1 pint)

Ingredients:

1/2 pound Swiss cheese finely grated

(ingredients continued on next page)

½ pound ricotta cheese

2 tablespoons skim milk

1 tablespoon grated onion

2 teaspoons chopped parsley

Method:

1. In a bowl, mix all of the ingredients together until well blended. Cheese spread should be of a soft spreading consistency. If not, add more skim milk.

Fresh Fruit

Use only the freshest and ripest fruits that are available. Strawberries and sliced pears provide different colors and shapes to the dish. Black or green grapes and sliced red apples are another eye-appealing combination. Portion fruit so that each guest will receive the equivalent of 1½ pieces of fruit. For example: 4 large strawberries and 2 quarters of a large pear, or 6 to 8 black grapes still on the stem with 2 quarters of an apple.

To Serve

On one-third of six luncheon plates, place a 1½ ounce scoop of cheese spread. It is attractive to pipe out the cheese spread through a pastry bag and star tube (see Working with a Pastry Bag, page 204) directly on the plate or into individual small crockery dishes that are then placed onto the plate. The cheese spread should preferably be served at room temperature or slightly chilled for easy spreading consistency. Place the fruit on the other third of the plate in an attractive arrangement. Just before serving, add the rye roll to plate that has been kept warm in a 150-degree oven. The asparagus puree soup may be served before, together, or after the fruit, cheese and roll plate.

I enjoy eating the entire meal together, and that is the way I serve it to my guests.

★ Traditional French Macaroons
(makes about 2 dozen)

Ingredients:

8 ounces almond paste

6 tablespoons confectioners' sugar

6 tablespoons granulated sugar

2 egg whites

Method:

1. In a mixing bowl, cream the almond paste with the confectioners' and granulated sugar.

2. Add the egg whites gradually until a smooth medium stiff paste is formed.

3. Bag out the mixture through a pastry bag and star tube (see Working with a Pastry Bag, page 204) on nonstick or lightly greased sheet pans.

4. Refrigerate for at least an hour.

5. Preheat oven to 400 degrees.

6. Right out of the refrigerator, bake in 400-degree oven for 15 to 20 minutes.

Menu
15

Salad Belvedere

(mixed greens, diced apples and diced beets)

Cheese Soufflé

Whole-Wheat Bread

★ Top Hats

(coffee ice cream in pastry shells with hot fudge sauce,
pistachio nuts and strawberries)

Salad Belvedere

Ingredients for salad dressing:

¼ cup safflower oil

¼ cup tarragon vinegar

⅓ cup unfiltered apple juice

2 tablespoons chopped parsley

Pinch of dry mustard

1/8 teaspoon black pepper

Ingredients for salad:

12 cups mixed salad greens (see About Preparing Salad Greens, page 202)

2 cups unpeeled Red Delicious apples

1 cup diced cooked beets

Method:

1. Combine all of the dressing ingredients and chill well.
2. Before serving, toss dressing gently with mixed greens, apples and beets. Reserve some beets and apples to garnish top of salad.

Cheese Soufflé

Every Saturday afternoon the cheese soufflé is traditionally served at Maine Chance. When I became the executive chef at Maine Chance, I designed a biweekly menu. I had cheese soufflé on the first Saturday alternated with a crabmeat crepe on the second Saturday. Although many of the diet changes I made were well received, I quickly learned not to tamper with certain Maine Chance traditions. The Saturday cheese soufflé has been served at Maine Chance for more than thirty-five years. So, if you are a guest staying for two weeks you can be certain that you will have cheese souffle both Saturday afternoons and heaven help the next chef who dares to alter this tradition!

The major difference between this cheese soufflé and conventional ones is the amount of fat. In most cheese soufflé recipes, a roux made with a good quantity of butter mixed with flour is used to thicken the milk. If you have had cheese soufflé and felt somewhat nauseated after eating it, most likely, you ate a little too much fat. The cheese by itself has enough fat to make the soufflé tender and creamy. Therefore, skim milk substitutes perfectly well for whole milk without affecting quality. I think you will find this souffle to be healthier, lighter and tastier than most butterfat-laden conventional cheese soufflés.

Ingredients:

Butter

Grated Parmesan cheese

1 cup skim milk

½ cup skim milk mixed with 3 tablespoons whole-wheat flour

1 cup grated Jarlsberg cheese (4 ounces)

1 cup grated mild Cheddar cheese (4 ounces)

5 egg yolks

¼ teaspoon cayenne pepper

8 egg whites

¼ teaspoon cream of tartar

Method:

(see To Make Grade "A" Soufflés, page 203)

1. Preheat oven to 350 degrees.
2. Prepare an 8-cup soufflé bowl by lightly buttering and sprinkling grated Parmesan cheese inside of bowl.
3. In a saucepan, heat 1 cup of milk until simmering. Add the well-blended mixture of ½ cup milk and 3 tablespoons flour to simmering milk and cook, stirring constantly, until mixture thickens. Remove from heat.
4. Add cheese and cayenne pepper. Egg yolks may be added as soon as the mixture is cool enough to prevent them from cooking. Mix thoroughly to obtain a smooth, lump-free sauce.
5. In a mixing bowl, beat the egg whites until foamy. Add cream of tartar and continue beating until egg whites are stiff and hold their shape, but still have a velvety appearance.
6. Fold cheese mixture into egg whites.
7. Pour mixture into the prepared soufflé bowl. Place in a pan of water and bake at 350 degrees for 1 hour and 15 minutes.

Whole-Wheat Bread

Ingredients:

2 cups milk

1 package dry or ⅔ ounce of compressed yeast

1 egg

2 tablespoons melted butter

(ingredients continued on next page)

¼ cup honey

1 teaspoon salt

6 cups unsifted stone-ground whole-wheat flour

1 beaten egg

Sesame seeds

Method:

1. Heat milk to about 100 degrees or the temperature of a warm bath.

2. Combine milk, yeast, egg, butter, honey and salt in a bowl. Let stand a few minutes to give yeast a chance to grow.

3. Add flour to make a soft and slightly sticky dough. The amount of flour to be added can vary depending on the flour's ability to absorb liquid. It is advisable to add the last cup of flour slowly until proper consistency.

4. Knead the dough by turning out onto a lightly floured worktable. Dust your hands with a little flour. Push your fingers into the dough and then press down with the heels of your hands, rolling the dough back and forth as you press. Keep kneading for about 5 minutes until the dough is elastic and satiny in texture.

5. Place dough in a lightly oiled bowl to prevent dough from sticking and cover with a damp towel or plastic wrap. Set bowl in a warm place, around 80 to 100 degrees. This can be near a warm stove or on a table in front of a sunny window.

6. When dough is double in bulk, deflate by punching it with your hand a few times.

7. Shape dough into two 8-inch buttered bread pans. Let dough rise again until double in bulk. Dough should rise until a nice rounded crest forms over the bread pan. While dough is rising, preheat oven to 350 degrees.

8. Brush top of bread gently with beaten egg. Sprinkle sesame seeds on top. Bake for about 50 minutes in 350-degree oven. Bread will be done when it shrinks from the side of the pan and a hollow sound is produced by tapping on it with your fingers.

★ Top Hats
(makes about 24 shells; freeze well)

Ingredients for pastry shells:

1 cup milk

¼ pound butter

1 cup and 2 tablespoons unbleached all-purpose flour

1 cup eggs

Method:

1. Preheat oven to 400 degrees.

2. In a heavy saucepan bring the milk and butter to a boil. Pour the flour all at once into the boiling mixture and cook the paste over low heat beating rapidly with a wooden spoon until the ingredients are thoroughly combined and the mixture cleanly leaves the sides of the pan and forms a ball. Remove pan from heat and let cool for a while.

3. Beat eggs one at a time into the mixture, beating well after each addition.

4. With a pastry bag and a No. 9 piping tube (see Working with a Pastry Bag, page 204) bag out round puffs about 2 inches in diameter on a nonstick or lightly greased baking pan. Bake at 400 degrees for about 25 to 30 minutes until golden brown and crisp.

Ingredients to make hot fudge sauce:

6 ounces unsweetened chocolate

¾ cup milk

1¼ cup granulated sugar

2 tablespoons butter

¼ cup Kahlua (coffee-flavored liqueur)

1 teaspoon vanilla extract

Method:

1. Melt chocolate in milk in a heavy metal saucepan over low heat or in a double boiler. Add sugar, stir and cook until dissolved. Remove from heat and add remaining ingredients.

Ingredients for final assembly:

6 pastry shells

Coffee ice cream

Hot fudge sauce

¼ cup unsalted pistachio nuts shelled, blanched in hot water to remove membrane and chopped.

1 pint whole washed strawberries

Method:

1. Remove top half of pastry shell. Place scoop of ice cream on lower half. Put top back on and place puffs on individual plates or on a large platter. Spoon hot fudge sauce on top, sprinkle with pistachio nuts and garnish with strawberries.

Menu 16

Salad Nicole

*(poached shrimp with cooked vegetable salad
and black grapes)*

Cleopatra's Shrimp Sauce

(yogurt-based sauce with tomato juice and dill weed)

Whole-Wheat Bread Sticks

★ Soufflé Grand Marnier

Salad Nicole

Salad Nicole is an elegant light meal that may be served on a large oval platter that can be prepared ahead, covered with plastic wrap and refrigerated. Serve Cleopatra's Shrimp Sauce on the side. Lemon wedges can be attractively presented in a bowl with a bouquet of fresh parsley in the center. The crunchy Whole-Wheat Bread Sticks make the meal complete: well rounded in tastes, colors, shapes and textures.

Poached Shrimp

Ingredients:

1 quart water

½ cup dry vermouth or dry white wine

1 onion finely sliced

2 stalks celery finely sliced

2 carrots finely sliced

½ teaspoon salt

½ teaspoon peppercorns

1 cup parsley sprigs

1 bay leaf

2½ pounds jumbo shrimp

Method:

1. In a large pot, simmer all of the ingredients together, excluding the shrimp, for one hour to make a court bouillon. Strain and reserve liquid.

2. Keep the court bullion at a simmer, add shrimp and cook, making sure the liquid stays at a simmer and is not allowed to boil. Boiling often produces a curled up, rubbery, tastless shrimp. Jumbo shrimp take about 7 minutes to cook providing they are not frozen. When done, the shrimp should no longer have a shiny, translucent raw look. They should be opaque, firm, not hard, and should hold their shape. Remove shrimp when done and let cool.

3. When cool enough to work with, peel the shell from the shrimp (if they are not peeled shrimp) and with a sharp knife remove the black vein down the back. Tail may be left on. Place shrimp in a covered container and refrigerate.

Cooked Vegetable Salad

Ingredients:

1 small head of cauliflower separated into small individual buds about ½-inch in diameter

1½ cups cut green beans, 1-inch long

1½ cups cut turnips about 1-inch long and ¼-inch in thickness

1½ cups cut carrots about 1-inch long and ¼-inch in thickness

1½ cups shelled green peas

Method:

1. In a quart of boiling water cook each vegetable one at a time. Vegetables should be cooked somewhat crunchy: not mushy and limp.
2. After each vegetable is cooked, remove with a skimmer or strainer and add the next one.
3. Place all of the cooked vegetables in a colander and let vegetables drain well. Save cooking liquid to use in Green Herbal Dressing.

Green Herbal Dressing

Ingredients:

1 bunch cleaned parsley

1 bunch cleaned watercress

8 peeled shallots or green onions

⅓ cup tarragon vinegar

⅓ cup safflower oil

⅔ cup vegetable stock from the cooked vegetables

1 coddled egg (cook room temperature egg for one minute in simmering water)

1 teaspoon dry mustard

1 teaspoon Worcestershire sauce

1 teaspoon salt

Method:

1. Place all of the ingredients in a blender. Blend well and refrigerate in a covered container.

Final Assembly for Salad Nicole

Ingredients:

Romaine, Boston or green leaf lettuce leaves for lining the platter
Cooked vegetables
Green Herbal Dressing
Cooked, cleaned and cooled shrimp
2 pounds black grapes washed and cut into bunches of 8 to 10 grapes

Method of platter assembly:

1. Line a 14 to 16-inch oval platter with the lettuce leaves, making sure that the outer edges of the leaves are along the border of the platter and the stalks face toward the center.
2. In a mixing bowl, toss the cooked vegetables with Green Herbal Dressing. Mound vegetables in the center of the platter making a neatly formed oval as in the shape of a half football.
3. Assemble shrimp in two neatly packed rows on both sides of the vegetables.
4. Complete platter by placing the bunches of grapes, stems down, at the ends of the platter.

Cleopatra's Shrimp Sauce

Ingredients:

½ cup yogurt
¼ cup mayonnaise
¼ cup tomato juice
1 tablespoon chili sauce
1/8 teaspoon Tabasco sauce
1 teaspoon fresh cut dill weed or ½ teaspoon dried dill weed

Method:

1. Mix all of the ingredients together and chill in refrigerator.

Whole-Wheat Bread Sticks
(makes 4 dozen)

Ingredients:

1½ cups water
1 tablespoon dry active yeast

(ingredients continued on next page)

1 tablespoon brown sugar

1 teaspoon salt

4 cups whole-wheat flour

1 egg, beaten

Poppyseeds

Sesame seeds

Onion salt

Method:

1. Preheat oven to 425 degrees.
2. Heat water to about 100 degrees or the temperature of a warm bath.
3. Dissolve the yeast, sugar and salt into the water in a mixing bowl.
4. Add flour until a fairly stiff dough is formed.
5. Turn dough onto a lightly floured board and knead until smooth and satiny. Divide dough into 48 pieces and roll each one into a cylinder ½-inch in diameter and 9-inches long. Place on lightly greased baking sheet.
6. Brush with beaten egg, and sprinkle bread sticks with poppyseeds and sesame seeds, forming alternating diagonal stripes. Sprinkle lightly with onion salt.
7. Bake 12 to 15 minutes in 425-degree oven until golden brown.

★ Soufflé Grand Marnier
(serves 6 people)

Ingredients for souffle:

(see To Make Grade "A" Soufflés, page 203)

4 tablespoons flour

½ cup milk

½ cup orange juice

½ cup granulated sugar

5 egg yolks

3 tablespoons butter

Grated peel of 1 orange

1 teaspoon pure vanilla extract

4 tablespoons Grand Marnier

7 egg whites

(ingredients continued on next page)

¼ teaspoon cream of tartar

1½ tablespoons sugar

Method:

1. Preheat oven to 350 degrees.

2. Butter and sugar an 8-cup soufflé bowl.

3. In a saucepan, mix the flour, milk, orange juice and ½ cup of sugar. Stir over high heat until mixture thickens and comes to a boil.

4. Remove from heat and let mixture cool for a few minutes. Add egg yolks, butter, grated orange peel, vanilla extract and Grand Marnier.

5. In a mixing bowl, beat the egg whites until foamy. Add the cream of tartar, 1½ tablespoons of sugar and keep beating until stiff peaks are formed.

6. Fold the egg whites into the egg yolk mixture. Pour mixture into prepared soufflé bowl. Place soufflé bowl in a pan of water. Bake soufflé in oven at 350 degrees for 1½ hours. Serve with sauce on the side.

Soufflé Sauce

Ingredients:

1 cup heavy cream

2 tablespoons light brown sugar

½ teaspoon pure vanilla extract

1 tablespoon Grand Marnier

Orange slices

Method:

1. Place all of the ingredients in a chilled whipping bowl. Beat until mixture thickens and soft peaks are formed. Serve sauce in chilled bowl surrounded with orange slices.

Menu
17

Hawaiian Chicken Salad

(chicken salad with cashew nuts stuffed in half a papaya, with fresh strawberries)

Poppyseed Toast

★The Black Mirror Cake

Hawaiian Chicken Salad

Ingredients:

2 cups cooked diced chicken or turkey

⅓ cup chopped toasted cashew nuts

⅓ cup diced celery

2 tablespoons diced red pepper

½ cup Yogurt Mayonnaise (see recipe below) or regular mayonnaise

1 tablespoon cider vinegar

Salt and pepper to taste

3 ripe papayas (if not available use 3 small melons)

1½ cups shredded lettuce

Romaine, Boston or green leaf lettuce leaves

1 pint strawberries

Sprigs of mint or parsley

Method:

1. Mix together the chicken, cashew nuts, celery, red pepper, mayonnaise and vinegar. Add salt and pepper to taste.

2. Cut papaya in half and remove seeds. Cut a small slice from the bottom of each half of papaya so that it will rest on a platter without tilting over.

3. Line the inside of each papaya half with shredded lettuce and place ⅓ to ½ cup of chicken salad on top. This may be done by using an ice cream scoop to get neat uniform mounds of chicken salad.

4. Line 6 luncheon plates with lettuce leaves. Place the prepared papaya in the center of the plate and garnish sides of plate with strawberries and mint sprigs or parsley sprigs.

Yogurt Mayonnaise

Ingredients:

2½ teaspoons plain gelatine

¼ cup water

3 egg yolks

½ cup safflower oil

1½ cups plain yogurt

(ingredients continued on next page)

¼ teaspoon dry mustard

1 teaspoon salt

Juice of 2 cloves garlic

Method:

1. Sprinkle gelatine over water and let stand for a few minutes to soften. Heat water slowly until gelatine is thoroughly dissolved.

2. In a bowl with a whip, in a blender or in a food processor, beat egg yolks and add oil slowly.

3. Add ¼ cup yogurt at a time to mixture.

4. Season with mustard, salt and garlic juice.

5. Add gelatine mixture. Refrigerate until mixture obtains a mayonnaise-like consistency.

Poppyseed Toast

Ingredients:

6 slices of whole-wheat bread

1 beaten egg

Poppyseeds

Onion salt

Method:

1. Preheat oven to 425 degrees.

2. Trim crust off bread and slice bread into three equal rectangular slices.

3. With a pastry brush, brush each slice with the beaten egg.

4. Sprinkle each piece lightly with poppyseeds and onion salt.

5. Bake in oven for about 10 minutes.

★ The Black Mirror Cake
(makes two 9-inch cakes)

The Black Mirror cake is a bittersweet chocolate cake with cherry preserves and amaretto liqueur. Legend has it that all those seeing their reflection in the cake's center will be guided on their path to inner beauty and wisdom throughout eternity.

Ingredients:

1¼ cups unbleached white flour

4 ounces finely ground almonds (grind almonds in a food processor or through a meat grinder)

½ pound unsalted butter

½ cup granulated sugar

¾ teaspoon salt

10 egg yolks

2 teaspoons vanilla extract

8 ounces bittersweet chocolate, melted

10 egg whites

½ cup granulated sugar

Method:

1. Preheat oven to 325 degrees.
2. Sift together the flour and ground almonds and set aside.
3. In a mixing bowl, cream the butter with ½ cup sugar and salt. Add egg yolks one at a time. Add vanilla extract. Mix in melted chocolate.
4. In a separate bowl, beat the egg whites until soft peaks begin to form. Add ½ cup sugar slowly and continue beating until firm peaks are just formed.
5. Fold the egg-white mixture into the chocolate mixture, then fold in the flour/nut mixture.
6. Distribute batter into two lightly greased or nonstick 9-inch cake pans. Bake at 325 degrees for 50 minutes. When done, let cool about 15 minutes, remove from cake pan and refrigerate.

Ingredients for frosting one 9-inch cake:

6 tablespoons amaretto liqueur

½ cup cherry preserves or strawberry preserves

12 ounces bittersweet chocolate

¾ cup yogurt at room temperature

2 ounces Baker's unsweetened chocolate, melted

1 tablespoon vegetable oil.

Method:

1. Cut top crust off cake and chop into fine crumbs. Set aside.
2. Cut cake in half. Sprinkle bottom half of cake with 3 tablespoons amaretto and then spread half of the preserves over it.

3. Mix melted bittersweet chocolate and yogurt together and spread about ¼ of the mixture over bottom half of cake.

4. Spread remaining preserves over top half of cake and place preserves side down over prepared bottom half of cake. Sprinkle with remaining amaretto.

5. Ice top and sides of cake with chocolate yogurt mixture and place cake crumbs around the side of cake.

6. Using a pastry bag and star tube (see Working with a Pastry Bag, page 204) pipe out a border around the top perimeter of cake. If the chocolate mixture is too runny, place bowl in ice water, keep mixing until proper consistency. At this point, the cake may be prepared well ahead of time. It may even be refrigerated or frozen. If refrigerated or frozen, make sure cake is at room temperature for serving.

7. Before serving, place cake on serving platter. Mix unsweetened Baker's chocolate with tablespoon of vegetable oil and pour into center of cake to make mirror. (The mirror will remain shiny for several hours, but in time will eventually crystalize.) Garnish side of cake with a few red marzipan roses and green leaves. (See next recipe.)

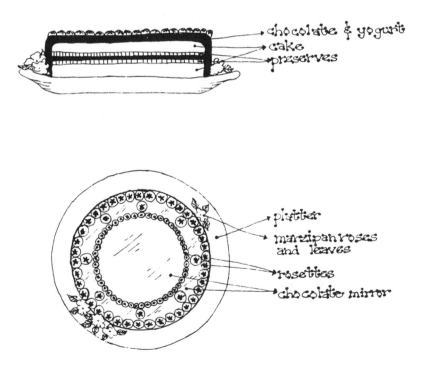

To Make Marzipan Roses

Ingredients:

Almond paste (purchased in most supermarkets and gourmet stores)

Red food coloring paste

Green food coloring paste
(Food coloring paste, preferred to liquid food coloring, may be purchased in cake decorating and restaurant supply stores.)

Method:

1. With a toothpick add a small touch of red food coloring to some almond paste and mix until the desired color is obtained. It is best not to mix completely to obtain the nuance of real roses.

2. Form a small 1-inch ice cream cone and place upside down on worktable.

3. Form ½-inch balls, then pinch between index finger and thumb to form petals. Work with a dampened cloth to prevent fingers from sticking to almond paste.

4. Place the first few petals closing in on top of cone. Work remaining petals down, out and around until rose is formed.

5. To make green leaves, follow method 1 using green food coloring. Pinch into desired leaves, place on worktable and score with a paring knife to make leaf veins.

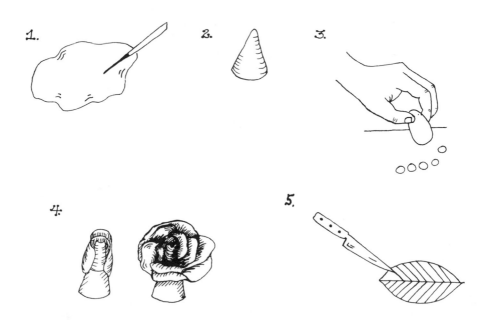

Menu
18

Consommé Parker

*(a clear transparent soup with sliced radishes,
sliced mushrooms and spinach leaves)*

Arizona Quiche

*(crustless chile pepper and cheese quiche with fresh fruit,
sliced tomato and alfalfa sprouts)*

★Aunt Selma's Rugalah

Consommé Parker

The French word "consommé" means "to finish," indicating that a proper consommé is a broth that is truly clarified or finished.

The process by which a consommé is obtained is termed clarification. The object of clarification is to extract all impurities and finely floating particles from a stock to produce a light, clear, transparent soup. Clarification of a consommé is accomplished by beating egg whites into cold stock, then heating it to a simmer for about 15 minutes. As the egg whites coagulate, they catch all of the minute particles in the stock. The mass of coagulated egg whites gradually rises to the surface leaving a crystal-clear liquid below.

Ingredients:

1½ quarts cold beef or chicken stock (see Stocks -- Les Fonds de Cuisine, page 197)

¾ pound chopped meat

2 egg whites

1 bunch cut green onions

Salt and white pepper to taste

¼ cup dry sherry

6 thinly sliced radishes

6 thinly sliced fresh mushrooms

Fresh spinach leaves

Method:

1. Combine the stock, chopped meat, egg whites and green onions in a heavy metal stock pot. Mix well.

2. Set on a moderate heat and stir from time to time until the stock reaches a simmer.

3. As soon as the stock begins to simmer, lower the heat and simmer very slowly without stirring for approximately 15 minutes. When the mass of coagulated egg whites rises to the top, remove from heat.

4. Let stand for about 5 minutes and then strain. This is done by gently removing the mass that has formed at the top with a skimmer. Then strain the clear liquid through paper towels or cheesecloth. With a ladle remove any fat on top of the consommé.

5. Season to taste with salt and white pepper. Add sherry.

6. Garnish each bowl of consommé with a few slices of radish, a few slices of mushroom and a few leaves of spinach.

Arizona Quiche

Many people relish a good quiche, while at the same time being suspicious of it. Their feelings are justified. A quiche can be a relatively high protein dish while at the same time be laden with a large amount of unnecessary fat from excessive usage of cream, butter, egg yolks, and shortening for the crust.

To make existing quiche recipes lighter, where the recipes call for cream or half-and-half use whole or 2% milk. Use a whole egg for every three egg yolks. Omit the butter from the recipes, and use whole-wheat bread crumbs for the crust as in the recipe for Arizona Quiche.

Ingredients:

½ tablespoon melted butter

1 beaten egg

¼ cup whole-wheat bread crumbs

1¼ cups grated Swiss cheese

1¼ cups grated Cheddar cheese

3 tablespoons diced green chile peppers

3 tablespoons diced pimiento

1 tablespoon chopped chives

½ teaspoon minced garlic

5 eggs

2 cups whole milk or 2% milk

⅓ teaspoon salt

6 beds of Boston, romaine or green leaf lettuce

Fresh fruit (melon, papaya, grapes, strawberries, apples)

1 pint alfalfa sprouts or radish sprouts or snow puff mushrooms or whatever

6 slices of tomato

French Dressing (see recipe on page 64)

Method:

1. Preheat oven to 400 degrees.

2. With a pastry brush, coat an 11-inch pie plate with butter. Refrigerate plate for a few minutes until butter turns solid. Brush a coating of beaten egg on top of butter. Sprinkle bread crumbs on top of egg coating. Turn plate upside down to remove excess bread crumbs. Bake the prepared plate in a 400-degree oven for 10 minutes. A thin whole-wheat crust will be produced that will not stick to the pie plate.

3. Mix the cheese with the chile peppers, pimientos, chives and garlic. Place mixture in pie plate. Mix the eggs, milk and salt together and pour over cheese mixture. Turn down oven to 350 degrees and bake for about 1 hour. When done, quiche should have a gelatine-like consistency and should not be hard and firm. Cut quiche into 8 pie-shaped pieces.

4. Place beds of lettuce on one half of 6 luncheon plates. Arrange fresh fruit, alfalfa sprouts and tomato slice on each bed of lettuce. Place hot piece of quiche on other half of plates and serve.

★ Aunt Selma's Rugalah
(makes 3 dozen)

Ingredients:

½ pound unsalted butter at room temperature

½ pound cream cheese at room temperature

6 tablespoons granulated sugar

1/8 teaspoon salt

2 eggs

1½ cups unbleached all-purpose flour

1 cup whole-wheat flour

1½ cups chopped pecans

1 cup light brown sugar

2 cups white raisins

1 tablespoon cinnamon

2 tablespoons brandy

1 cup strawberry preserves

1 beaten egg

Method:

1. In a mixing bowl, cream together the butter, cream cheese, sugar and salt. Add eggs one at a time. Add both flours and mix until a sticky dough is formed. Divide dough into three pieces; refrigerate for about one hour.

2. Mix pecans, sugar, raisins, cinnamon and brandy together.

3. Flour worktable and rolling pin liberally. Roll out a piece of the dough about 24 by 6 inches and approximately ¼-inch in thickness. Spread one-third of strawberry preserves over the surface of the rolled out dough. Sprinkle one-third of the raisin/nut mixture on top. Roll dough up lengthwise and cut forming 2½-inch pieces. Place on

greased or nonstick sheet pan. Repeat procedure with remaining two pieces of dough.

4. With a pastry brush, paint each piece of Rugalah with beaten egg. Bake in preheated 375-degree oven for about 35 minutes until golden brown. After baking, while still hot, remove Rugalah from baking pan as soon as possible.

Menu 19

Surprise Salad
(assorted greens, cottage cheese, apples, beets, garbanzo beans on top of a poached peach half)

Arden Dressing

Blueberry Muffins

Surprise Salad

Ingredients:

6 freshly poached peach halves (simmer in apple juice until tender) or 6 canned peach halves

12 cups mixed salad greens (see About Preparing Salad Greens, page 202)

6 cups spinach leaves

1 quart cottage cheese

2 large Red Delicious apples

¼ cup apple juice mixed with 1 teaspoon lemon juice

18 small round freshly cooked or canned beets (reserve 1 teaspoon beet juice for Arden Dressing)

1 17-ounce can garbanzo beans

Method:

1. Place a peach half on the bottom of 6 individual 1-quart capacity salad bowls. Cover peaches with 2 cups of salad greens and line the top of the bowls with spinach leaves.

2. Place a scoop, approximately 3 ounces, of cottage cheese in the center of each bowl.

3. Cut apples in half, core and cut into ¼-inch thick slices. Dip slices into apple-lemon juice mixture to retard browning. Place 3 slices around each scoop of cottage cheese.

4. On the outside and in between apple slices place 3 beets on each salad. Sprinkle garbanzo beans between beets.

Arden Dressing

Ingredients:

½ cup yogurt

½ cup mayonnaise

½ cup French Dressing (see recipe on page 64)

1 teaspoon chopped dill weed, preferably fresh

1 teaspoon beet juice

Method:

1. In a bowl mix the yogurt and mayonnaise together. Add remaining ingredients. Chill well before serving.

Blueberry Muffins
(makes 16 muffins)

Ingredients:

2¼ cups whole-wheat flour

¼ cup cornmeal

¾ teaspoon baking powder

½ tablespoon baking soda

½ teaspoon salt

½ cup buttermilk

½ cup safflower oil

⅔ cup honey

4 eggs

1 teaspoon vanilla extract

2 cup fresh or frozen blueberries

Method:

1. Preheat oven to 375 degrees.
2. In a bowl combine the flour, cornmeal, baking powder, baking soda and salt. Mix well with a wire whip.
3. Add the buttermilk, oil, honey, eggs and vanilla. Stir ingredients until blended. Fold in blueberries.
4. Scoop or spoon batter into nonstick or greased muffin tins three-fourths of the way full.
5. Bake in oven for approximately 25 minutes at 375 degrees.

Menu 20

**Gingered Duck or Chicken Salad
with Shitaki Mushrooms
and Chinese Rice Sticks**

Served with Fresh Fruit

Gingered Duck or Chicken Salad
with Shitaki Mushrooms
and Chinese Rice Sticks

Ingredients:

1 3- to 3½-pound uncooked duck (substitute chicken if you prefer)

1 red bell pepper

1 green bell pepper

8 large Shitaki mushrooms

3 ounces Chinese rice sticks

1 tablespoon finely diced ginger

1½ tablespoons cut chives

1 cup sliced water chestnuts

¼ cup Chinese rice vinegar

¼ cup soy sauce

¼ cup strong-tasting chicken stock or consommé

1 teaspoon sesame or peanut oil

1 head of fresh spinach

1 head of Radicchio lettuce (A relatively new purple-colored lettuce
    from Europe now grown in California and available in some U.S.
    cities. Substitute red cabbage if not available.)

1 cup finely grated carrot

1 pint fresh strawberries uncapped

1 small pineapple cut into slices with rind left on

Method:

1. Remove skin from duck and bone out as much meat as possible; cut
   into thin slivers and place in a large mixing bowl.
2. Cut bell peppers and Shitaki mushrooms into very thin 2-inch-long
   slivers. Place in bowl with duck and add Chinese rice sticks.
3. Bring 2 quarts of water to a rolling boil, pour over ingredients in
   bowl. Let stand for 10 minutes then drain in a colander.
4. Place drained ingredients back into mixing bowl, add ginger,
   chives, water chestnuts, rice vinegar, soy sauce, chicken stock or
   consommé and oil. Toss together.
5. Lay out a bed of spinach leaves on 6 luncheon plates with spinach
   stems toward the center of plates. Form cups with 3 to 4 Radicchio
   lettuce leaves. Place cups on spinach leaves and fill with duck salad.
   Garnish top of salad with shredded carrot. Garnish side of plate with
   strawberries and pineapple.

Menu
21

Chilled Gazpacho Soup

**Open-Faced Tuna or Egg Salad
Sandwich Plate**

★ Linzertorte

(almond coffee cake)

Chilled Gazpacho Soup

Russian Borsch (beet soup); Turkey's Cucik (yogurt and cucumber soup); Vienna's Hideg Meggylves (sour cherry soup); France's Vichyssoise (leek and potato soup) all have two things in common. They are all cold soups and none surpass the Spanish Gazpacho (tomato vegetable soup) in popularity.

Gazpacho soup's modern-day popularity no doubt stems from the fact that it is a low-calorie nutritious soup. Like everyone's metabolism, no two gazpacho recipes are exactly alike. Almonds, grapes, white wine, pitted cherries, croutons and stale bread have all been used in gazpacho soup. Use this recipe as just one example, and let your taste buds and your imagination be your guide.

Ingredients:

2 large tomatoes peeled and seeded

2 cucumbers peeled and seeded

1 green pepper

4 green onions

1 clove minced garlic

2 cups V-8 juice

1 cup beef stock or canned beef consommé (see Stocks -- Les Fonds de Cuisine, page 197)

4 tablespoons red wine vinegar

¼ teaspoon Tabasco sauce

2 tablespoons chopped parsley

Method:

1. Dice 1 tomato, 1 cucumber, ½ green pepper and 2 green onions. Set the diced vegetables aside.

2. Place all of the remaining ingredients in a blender. Blend until a thickened puree is produced. Add the diced vegetables, chill well, preferably overnight, before serving.

Open-Faced Tuna or Egg Salad Sandwich Plate

Ingredients for tuna or egg salad:

1 13-ounce can white albacore tuna or use 12 hard-boiled eggs to make egg salad

2 hard-boiled eggs (for tuna salad)

2 stalks celery finely diced

(ingredients continued on next page)

1 small peeled carrot finely chopped

½ to ¾ cup Yogurt Mayonnaise (see recipe on page 83) or regular mayonnaise

1 tablespoon lemon juice

Method:

1. Flake tuna into small pieces or chop eggs into small chunks. Add the remaining ingredients together. Taste for seasoning and refrigerate until ready to assemble plates.

Ingredients for the plates:

6 slices whole-wheat bread

1 pint alfalfa sprouts

Prepared tuna or egg salad

6 radish roses (Cut radish roses by making perpendicular cuts to form petals around the outside of the radish. Place in icewater to open petals.)

6 wedges of watermelon or 6 half pieces of Red Delicious apples with cores removed. (Soak apples in lemon juice and water for a minute to prevent them from turning brown.)

18 dill pickle chips

6 sprigs parsley

6 lemon wedges

Method to assemble plate:

1. Cut out slices of whole-wheat bread into six 4-inch rounds. If you do not have round cutters, use the empty can from the tuna.

2. Cover bread with some alfalfa sprouts and scoop a 3-ounce portion of tuna or egg salad on top of sprouts.

3. Garnish plates with a radish rose, a wedge of watermelon or half an apple, 3 pickle chips, a parsley sprig and a lemon wedge.

★ Linzertorte

Ingredients:

1 cup unsalted butter

1 cup unbleached pastry flour

1½ cups grated unpeeled almonds

¼ cup granulated sugar

(ingredients continued on next page)

½ teaspoon salt

¼ teaspoon ground cloves

¼ teaspoon cinnamon

2 egg yolks

1 cup raspberry jam

½ egg white

Confectioners' sugar

Slivered almonds

Method:

1. Crumble butter into flour. Add grated almonds. Mix sugar with salt, ground cloves, cinnamon, and egg yolks. Knead dough until smooth and well blended.

2. Turn two-thirds of dough in a 9-inch, ungreased cake pan with removable bottom. Press over bottom and halfway up sides. Spread with raspberry jam.

3. Roll egg-sized balls of remaining dough between palms to make long rolls about a third to a half inch in diameter and about 8 inches long. Put rolls on baking sheet, chill until firm.

4. Using a spatula, lift rolls and arrange lattice-style over jam. Fasten to dough around rim of pan by pressing lightly. Brush with slightly beaten egg white.

5. Bake on lower shelf of a preheated oven at 325 degrees for about 1 hour and 15 minutes. Set pan on rack and partly cool cake before removing rim of pan.

6. Before serving sprinkle cake with confectioners' sugar and, if desired, slivered almonds.

Menu
22

Spinach Salad

Basket of Assorted Crackers

Cold Poached King Salmon Steaks

Sauce Verte

**Honey Broiled Grapefruit
with Mandarin Orange Sections**

Spinach Salad

Ingredients for dressing:

1 cup chicken consommé or chicken stock (see Stocks -- Les Fonds de Cuisine, page 197)

½ cup red wine vinegar

½ cup safflower oil

2 cloves minced garlic

2 tablespoons chopped parsley

2 tablespoons grated Parmesan cheese

2 teaspoons granulated sugar

½ teaspoon salt

½ teaspoon pepper

Pinch of dry mustard

Ingredients for salad:

3 heads fresh spinach

9 large mushrooms washed and thinly sliced

3 chopped pieces of crisp cooked bacon

1 chopped hard-boiled egg

Method:

1. Make dressing by mixing all of the dressing ingredients together. Chill well.

2. Tear spinach from stems, wash and dry well. Cover with a damp towel or plastic wrap and chill in refrigerator.

3. Before serving, pour dressing over spinach, add mushrooms, bacon and egg. Toss gently to prevent bruising the salad greens. Serve in chilled salad bowl.

Basket of Assorted Crackers

The crackers will add the needed "crunch" to this meal. Just for a change, let's make it easy for both of us. You buy the assorted crackers (good whole-grain ones) and I will not have to bother writing recipes for assorted crackers! O.K.?

Cold Poached King Salmon Steaks

Ingredients:

6 5-ounce salmon steaks, ¾ to 1 inch in thickness

1½ quarts water

1 cup dry vermouth or dry white wine

1 onion, sliced

2 stalks finely sliced celery

2 carrots finely sliced

½ teaspoon salt

½ teaspoon peppercorns

1 cup parsley sprigs

1 small bay leaf

Method:

1. In a large pot, simmer all of the ingredients, excluding the salmon, for 1 hour to make a court bouillon. Strain, reserve liquid and bring to a simmer.
2. Preheat oven to 350 degrees.
3. Place salmon steaks in bottom of a lightly buttered baking pan. Pour simmering court bouillon over fish and bake, covered with aluminum foil, for 25 minutes. Let pan cool for a while at room temperature. Then refrigerate overnight, letting fish remain in court bouillon.
4. Before serving, gently remove fish from court bouillon and clean with a pastry brush dipped in water. Salmon steaks may be attractively arranged on a platter with lemon wedges and parsley sprigs on the outside of the platter and a lemon flower basket in the center of the platter.

Sauce Verte

Ingredients:

1½ cups Yogurt Mayonnaise (see recipe on page 83) or 1 cup yogurt mixed with ½ cup regular mayonnaise

¼ cup skim milk

½ tablespoon lemon juice

1 tablespoon chopped chives

1 tablespoon chopped parsley

1 tablespoon dill weed

Method:

1. Mix all of the ingredients together.

Honey Broiled Grapefruit
with Mandarin Orange Sections

Ingredients:

3 grapefruit

3 teaspoons Grand Marnier or other orange-flavored liqueur

3 teaspoons honey

6 black grapes

2 mandarin oranges peeled, sectioned and seeded. (Use canned if fresh are not available.)

Method:

1. Preheat broiler.
2. Halve the grapefruit and cut a small slice from the bottom so that they will rest on a plate without tilting over. Separate the sections from the membrane with a grapefruit knife. Spoon ½ teaspoon Grand Marnier and ½ teaspoon honey over each half grapefruit.
3. Broil the grapefruit 6 inches from heat for about 5 minutes or until the tops are golden brown.
4. Garnish grapefruit with a black grape in the center. Encircle each grape with 3 or 4 mandarin orange sections.

Menu
23

Crenshaw Melon

Poached Chicken Breasts Dolphin
*(poached chicken breasts on a bed of saffron rice,
garnished with broccoli and radish roses)*

Cup of Custard

Crenshaw Melon

Ingredients:

6 cut wedges from a ripe Crenshaw melon

6 large strawberries

6 wedges of lime

Method:

1. Cut a small slice from the bottom of each wedge of melon so that it will rest on a plate without tilting over.
2. Place a strawberry and a wedge of lime in the center of the melon wedge. Serve slightly chilled or at room temperature.

Poached Chicken Breasts Dolphin

The entire entree is most attractive when arranged and presented on a large oval platter. To some degree Poached Chicken Breasts Dolphin is a take-off on the famous Spanish dish Arroz con Pollo (chicken with rice). The name "Dolphin" has nothing to do with the mammal that swims in the ocean. The dish is named after Anthony Dolphin, a fine sous-chef, with whom I have the pleasure of working with at Maine Chance.

Poached Chicken Breasts

Ingredients:

3 whole breasts from 2½ to 3-pound fryers

1 cup chicken stock or canned chicken consommé (see Stocks -- Les Fonds de Cuisine, page 197)

1 lemon

Butter

Salt

Parchment paper or aluminum foil

Method:

1. Slip fingers between skin and flesh and pull off skin. Cut the meat along the breastbone with a sharp paring or boning knife while using your other hand to separate the meat from the breastbone. Continue to separate and cut until the meat from one side of the breast separates in one piece. Trim off any fat or jagged edges. Bone out other side of breast in the same manner.

2. Lay out the boned and trimmed breasts on a lightly buttered baking pan. Squeeze the juice of a lemon over the breasts, sprinkle lightly with salt and add the chicken stock.

3. Cover breasts with buttered parchment paper or aluminum foil. Bake in a preheated 325-degree oven for about 15 to 20 minutes.
    The trick to cooking chicken breasts so that they are juicy and tender is not to overcook them. As soon as the breast springs back with gentle resilience and there is still the slightest trace of pink left in the center of the breast, they are ready. Any further cooking will begin to toughen the meat. It is for this reason I prefer to use parchment paper instead of aluminum foil making it easier to check the doneness of the chicken breasts. Save cooking juice from pan to baste cooked breasts and broccoli before serving on prepared platter.

Saffron Rice

Saffron is a crocus-like flower native to Asia Minor, that was introduced to Spain by the Moors. People buying saffron for the first time are often astounded to pay so much for so little of one of the world's most expensive spices. But it is understandable when we know how it is derived. The spice taken from the saffron plant is not the seed, a leaf, nor the root, but a very small part of the flower, the stigma, part of the pistil, extending out to receive the pollen. Each blossom has three stigmas, and it takes approximately a quarter of a million stigmas to make one pound of spice. Fortunately a little saffron goes a long way.

Ingredients:

4 cups chicken stock or canned chicken consommé (see Stocks -- Les Fonds de Cuisine, page 197)

½ teaspoon whole saffron (not ground)

1 bay leaf

1 clove garlic

1 tablespoon olive oil

1 small onion finely chopped

1 green pepper finely diced

1 red pepper finely diced

2 cups long grain brown rice

Method:

1. Simmer the stock with the saffron, bay leaf and clove of garlic for about 20 minutes.

2. In a skillet sauté the onion and peppers in the oil until onions turn

translucent. Rinse rice with cold water and drain well. Add rice and cook, stirring until rice turns opaque.

3. Strain saffron, bay leaf and garlic out, discard, and add the stock to the rice in skillet. Cover skillet and cook over low heat for about 50 to 60 minutes until the rice has absorbed all of the liquid.

Broccoli
(serves 6)

Ingredients:

3 pounds broccoli

Method:

(See About Cooking Vegetables, page 200.)

1. Wash broccoli and discard the coarse leaves and lower part of the stalks. Halve or quarter the bunches lengthwise depending on their size to make them all no more than ½ inch in diamater at the base. Steam or boil until the vegetables are tender but still crunchy with a bright green color.

Radish Roses

Ingredients:

6 large radishes

Method:

1. Make perpendicular cuts to form petals around the outside of the radish. Place in ice water to open petals.

Final Assembly of Platter

Mound the rice on a large oval platter. Divide broccoli into 6 equal portions and place 3 portions on each side of the platter, stems down. Place the chicken breasts in the center of the platter, garnish with radish roses and strain the liquid left from the baking pan over the chicken breasts. Platter may also be garnished with an apple bird (see diagram of apple bird on page 160).

Cup of Custard

Ingredients:

2 cups whole milk

4 eggs

¼ cup granulated sugar

1 teaspoon pure vanilla extract

6 washed and drained canned pitted Bing cherries

⅓ cup heavy cream

1 tablespoon brown sugar

¼ cup brandy

¼ cup brown sugar

6 pecan halves

Method:

1. Preheat oven to 350 degrees.
2. Scald milk in a saucepan. In a bowl, with a wire whip, beat eggs with ¼ cup granulated sugar. Add scalded milk and vanilla extract; mix well. Distribute mixture evenly into six 6-ounce custard cups.
3. Place a Bing cherry into each custard cup. Place cups in a baking pan and fill pan with about 1 inch of water. Bake in 350-degree oven for about 35 to 45 minutes until custard coagulates to a gelatine-like consistency. Take care not to overbake custard; making it a firm rubbery product. When done, let cool for a while, remove cups from pan, cover with plastic wrap and refrigerate.
4. In a chilled bowl, beat heavy cream and 1 tablespoon brown sugar until stiff peaks are formed. Pipe out a small rosette of whipped cream with a pastry bag and star tube on each cooled cup of custard. (See Working with a Pastry Bag, page 204.)
5. In a saucepan, bring ¼ cup brandy and ¼ cup brown sugar to a boil. Ignite brandy with a match or by tipping pan over a gas burner. Let burn for 30 seconds. Before flame dies out, cover saucepan with a lid to extinguish flame. The idea is to reduce the alcoholic content of the brandy. Remove from heat and let cool for a while.
6. Place a teaspoon of warm brandy sauce on top of each prepared cup of custard and top whipped cream rosettes with pecan halves.

Menu
24

Clark Salad

*(mixed greens, artichokes, sliced radishes
in dill dressing)*

Lobster Tails Fra Diavolo

Coco-Lemon Ices

Clark Salad

Ingredients:

2 teaspoons fresh chopped dill weed or 1 teaspoon dried dill weed
French Dressing (see recipe on page 64)
10 cups mixed greens (see About Preparing Salad Greens, page 202)
10 thinly sliced red radishes
12 freshly cooked or canned baby artichokes cut in half

Method:

1. Add dill to French Dressing.
2. Before serving, toss greens with radishes and artichoke hearts, saving some radishes and hearts to garnish the top of the salad. Serve in a large chilled salad bowl or in individual chilled plates or bowls.

Lobster Tails Fra Diavolo

Gastronomically speaking, I would have to go along with using fresh lobster, including all of its parts, for best results. I don't believe any seafood, poultry, meat or vegetable can replace its fresh counterpart in quality. Yet many people shy away from cooking fresh lobster because it is somewhat difficult to handle, and lobsters are not particularly the most attractive creatures. Oftentimes they are unavailable in many markets. It is for this reason I have called for using frozen lobster tails -- an easy, always available alternative.

Ingredients:

8 6- to 8-ounce lobster tails, thawed
1½ tablespoons olive oil
3 cups sliced mushrooms
½ cup chopped onion
1 tablespoon finely chopped garlic
2 cups Italian plum tomatoes, peeled and chopped
3 cups dry white wine
1 tablespoon chopped basil
1 tablespoon chopped oregano
¼ teaspoon crushed hot red pepper
Salt to taste
1 tablespoon chopped parsley
1 pound cooked spinach macaroni
6 lemon wedges

Method:

1. Deshell lobster and cut into quarters. In a large skillet sauté lobster in ½ tablespoon olive oil over medium high heat. Cook them 2 to 3 minutes, turning frequently. Remove with a slotted spoon when tails become somewhat crisp on the outside but not completely cooked through. Set aside.

2. Add another ½ tablespoon of oil to skillet and sauté the sliced mushrooms until slices are slightly browned but still crisp. Set aside.

3. Add remaining ½ tablespoon oil to skillet and sauté onions until loose and transparent. Add garlic, tomatoes, wine, basil, oregano and red pepper. Stirring occasionally, boil sauce until it is reduced to about 3 cups.

4. Add lobster, cover skillet and cook for about 7 minutes on a moderate heat until lobster is completely cooked through. Take care not to overcook them. Taste sauce for seasoning and add salt if necessary.

5. Stir parsley and mushrooms into the lobster mixture to heat through. Spoon entire mixture over macaroni on a large heated platter and garnish with lemon wedges.

Coco-Lemon Ices

Ingredients:

12-ounce can natural lemon flavor pink lemonade

8 ounces water

6 ounces Coco Lopez cream of coconut

¼ cup kirsch cherry liqueur

Ice

6 thin slices of lime

6 fresh pitted Bing cherries or 6 canned pitted Bing cherries that have been well drained

Method:

1. In a 6-cup blender, add the lemonade, water, Coco Lopez, kirsch and enough ice to fill blender almost to top. Blend well until a thick slushy mixture is obtained. Pour into a pan, cover and freeze overnight.

2. Using a small ice cream scoop, scoop a round ball of the ice into 6 stemmed cocktail glasses. (At Maine Chance I use a 1-ounce scoop for dieters. It is enough to refresh and satisfy the sweet tooth). Garnish with a thin slice of lime placed on the inside rim of each glass. Place a Bing cherry in the center of each lime slice.

Menu 25

Garcia Salad

*(Mexican-style salad with shredded lettuce
and diced vegetables)*

Crepes Elizabeth

*(turkey and spinach filled whole-wheat crepes
served with a carrot sauce)*

Hot Blueberry Cobbler
with Honey Yogurt

Garcia Salad

The Garcia Salad is a Mexican-style salad. Mexican cuisine, like Mexican art, is colorful and is gaining much recognition. What makes this salad unusual is that the lettuce is shredded with a knife instead of torn apart or cut into pieces. It is also served in a mound on a platter, instead of in a salad bowl. The greens are garnished with a mixture of small-cut vegetables producing a bright, lively looking salad.

Ingredients:

1 head iceberg lettuce

1 head romaine or green leaf lettuce

½ cup sliced celery

2 tomatoes diced

½ cup sliced green onions

½ cup sliced pitted black olives

1 pint alfalfa sprouts

French Dressing (see recipe on page 64)

Method:

1. Shred iceberg and romaine lettuce and place in a mound in the center of a large round or oval platter. Sprinkle celery, tomatoes, onions and olives over top of lettuce mound. Encircle the mound with alfalfa sprouts.
2. Serve salad with dressing on the side.

Crepes Elizabeth

Ingredients for crepes:

3 eggs

¾ cup whole-wheat flour

1 cup milk

¼ teaspoon salt

Method:

1. Combine all of the ingredients in a large bowl and beat with a wire whip or in a blender until smooth. Refrigerate for at least two hours. It may be left overnight.
2. On a medium high burner, heat a nonstick 8-inch frypan until it is hot enough so that a drop of water bounces around the pan.
3. Pour a very thin layer of batter in skillet, approximately one ounce.

Rotate skillet to make sure batter covers entire bottom of skillet.

4. When the crepe is set (becomes loose from the pan), and begins to show brown edges, turn crepe on other side and cook for about 15 seconds. Set crepes aside.

Filling for Crepes

Ingredients:

2 tablespoons butter

¼ cup chopped shallots or green onions

2 tablespoons whole-wheat flour

1 cup milk or 2% milk

3 heads spinach, cleaned and chopped

1 egg

1 cup sliced water chestnuts

2 cups cooked chunk turkey or chicken

1 teaspoon salt

¼ teaspoon cayenne pepper

Method:

1. In a saucepan, sauté shallots or green onions in butter until soft and translucent. Add flour, stir and cook for a minute. Add milk slowly and keep stirring to prevent lumps from forming. Cook until milk comes to a boil and thickens.

2. In a large kettle of boiling water, blanch spinach for one minute, then drain well by pressing down on spinach with your hands in a colander. Add spinach and remaining ingredients to milk mixture.

3. Place 3 to 4 ounces of spinach on ends of crepes. Roll crepes up and place on a nonstick or lightly greased baking pan, making sure there is at least a half-inch space between crepes.

Carrot Sauce

Ingredients:

1½ cups milk

1½ cups chicken stock or chicken consommé (see Stocks -- Les Fonds de Cuisine, page 197)

3 cups peeled and chopped carrots

Salt

White pepper

Method:

1. Combine the milk, stock or consommé, and carrots in a saucepan. Bring to a simmer and cook for about 20 minutes until carrots are tender.

2. Puree mixture in a blender and season to taste with salt and pepper. Keep hot.

Final Assembly of Crepes

Ingredients:

½ tablespoon melted butter

6 large mushrooms

6 filled spinach crepes on baking pan

Hot carrot sauce

½ tablespoon chopped chives

Method:

1. Preheat oven to 400 degrees.

2. Brush melted butter on fluted mushrooms and place them on the same baking pan with the crepes. Bake pan in oven for 15 to 20 minutes.

3. Align crepes on a warm oval silver or china platter. Pour hot carrot sauce over crepes and sprinkle with chopped chives. Place mushroom caps on top center of each crepe and serve.

Hot Blueberry Cobbler with Honey Yogurt

Ingredients:

2 pints blueberries

2 tablespoons granulated sugar

1 teaspoon grated lemon rind

⅓ cup water

4 tablespoons butter, at room temperature

½ cup whole-wheat flour

½ cup rolled oats

¼ cup brown sugar

¼ teaspoon cinnamon

(ingredients continued on next page)

1/8 teaspoon almond extract

2 cups plain yogurt

Honey

Method:

1. Preheat oven to 375 degrees.

2. Combine the berries, granulated sugar, lemon rind and water in a saucepan. Bring ingredients to a boil and simmer for 2 minutes.

3. Meanwhile, combine the butter, flour, oats, brown sugar, cinnamon, and almond extract. Work with your hands until mixture is crumbly.

4. Transfer blueberries to a large shallow heatproof casserole or individual casserole dishes. Sprinkle crumbs over berries. Bake about 30 minutes until browned.

5. Mix yogurt with honey until desired sweetness. Serve on the side with the hot blueberry cobbler.

Menu
26

Pineapple Watercress Juice

Sautéed Bay Scallops

Eggplant Creole

**Braised Romaine Lettuce
with Apples and Currants**

Saratoga Chips
(the original fried potato chip)

★ Strawberry Raspberry Hemisphere

Pineapple Watercress Juice

Ingredients:

24 ounces chilled unsweetened pineapple juice

1 cup diced pineapple

1 cup watercress sprigs

Method:

1. Purée ingredients in blender and serve in chilled cocktail glasses.

Sautéed Bay Scallops

Ingredients:

1½ pounds bay scallops

1 tablespoon butter

1½ tablespoons Eight Seasons Salt (see recipe on page 55)

1 lemon cut into 6 wedges

1 lime cut into 6 wedges

Fresh parsley sprig and/or fresh basil leaves

Method:

1. Over a medium high heat in a large nonstick skillet cook scallops in butter and seasoning salt until the center of scallops lose their shiny appearance. Take care not to overcrowd the skillet so that the scallops will have room to roll around the pan cooking evenly. Therefore it may be necessary to cook scallops, depending on the size of your skillet, in a few batches. Cooking time is only a minute or two.

2. Roll out scallops onto a heated serving platter or dinner plates, garnish with lemon and lime wedges, parsley sprigs and/or basil leaves.

Eggplant Creole

Ingredients:

1 tablespoon olive oil

1 small diced onion

2 stalks celery diced

1 diced green pepper

2 cloves chopped garlic

(ingredients continued on next page)

1 teaspoon basil

½ teaspoon thyme

1 tablespoon chopped parsley

1½ cups tomato sauce

2 tomatoes peeled and chopped (prick the skin, then plunge tomatoes into boiling water for 10 seconds to peel skin)

1 large unpeeled eggplant cut into 1-inch cubes

1 teaspoon lemon juice

Salt and pepper to taste

Method:

1. Add the oil, onions, celery and green pepper to a large skillet with a tight-fitting cover. Stir and cook over a medium high heat until vegetables are wilted.

2. Add the remaining ingredients, cover skillet and cook over low heat for about 45 minutes until eggplant is tender. Be sure to stir mixture on occasion. Add salt and pepper to taste.

Braised Romaine Lettuce with Apples and Currants

Ingredients:

3 heads romaine lettuce

¼ teaspoon cayenne pepper

1½ cups strong-flavored chicken stock or canned consomme (see Stocks -- Les Fonds de Cuisine, page 197)

1 Red Delicious apple

2 tablespoons dried currants

1 cup apple juice

Method:

1. Discard any bruised leaves and cut romaine lettuce in half lengthwise.

2. In a large pot of boiling water, blanche lettuce until leaves are wilted. Remove from water and set aside in a casserole.

3. Add cayenne pepper to chicken stock and pour into casserole; cover and refrigerate overnight.

4. Cut apple into ¼-inch slices. Pour apple juice into a saucepan, add apple slices and currants.

5. Before serving, heat lettuce in casserole and heat apple slices and currant in saucepan. Serve romaine lettuce on plates or platter topped with sliced apples and currants.

Saratoga Chips

Ingredients:

2 cups frying oil

1½ pounds baking potatoes

Method:

1. In a heavy metal skillet heat oil to 375 degrees.
2. Scrub potatoes and cut into very thin slices leaving the peel on. Fry slices in 375-degree oil until golden brown, remove and drain on paper towels. Keep warm in a low-temperature oven until serving.

★ Strawberry Raspberry Hemisphere

The Strawberry Raspberry Hemisphere is a raspberry mousse that is molded in a 2½-quart round mixing bowl to give the dessert the hemispherical shape. When unmolded, the mousse is placed on a baked flan crust that has been filled with sliced strawberries. The mousse is then decorated with more strawberries and whipped cream.

The Hemisphere will serve 12 to 16 people. It makes for an elegant light dessert to end a delicious meal or may be used for a special occasion by simply writing on the mousse "Happy Anniversary," or whatever the occasion may be.

To Make Raspberry Mousse

Ingredients:

2 10-ounce packages sweetened frozen raspberries

2½ packages Knox unflavored gelatine

2 cups heavy cream

6 eggs separated

1½ cups sugar

1 tablespoon Grand Marnier

3 tablespoons lemon juice

Method:

1. Thaw raspberries and force through a strainer to form a purée and

remove seeds. There should be approximately 1½ cups of puree.

2. In a saucepan, add gelatine to ½ cup raspberry purée. Stir over low heat until gelatine is completely dissolved. Set aside and keep warm.

3. In a chilled mixing bowl whip the heavy cream until stiff peaks are formed. Set aside in the refrigerator.

4. In a mixing bowl beat the 6 egg yolks on high speed adding 1 cup of sugar gradually over a 3-minute period. Continue beating while adding gradually the remaining 1 cup of raspberry purée. Add Grand Marnier, lemon juice and gelatine mixture. Set bowl aside.

5. In a mixing bowl whip the egg whites, adding remaining ½ cup sugar gradually until stiff peaks are just formed.

6. Fold egg whites into egg yolk mixture. Fold in whipped cream. Pour mixture into a 2½-quart round mixing bowl that has been lightly oiled. Refrigerate for at least 3 hours.

To Make Flan Crust

Ingredients:
½ pound sweet butter

⅓ cup sugar

¼ teaspoon salt

2 egg yolks

1½ teaspoons pure vanilla extract

2 cups unsifted unbleached pastry flour

Method:
1. Preheat oven to 375 degrees.

2. In a mixing bowl cream butter, sugar and salt together. Add egg yolks one at a time. Add vanilla extract. Add flour and continue to mix until a dough has formed.

3. Working with your hands, line a greased 11-inch flan mold with a removable bottom. Crimp a 1-inch crust around the perimeter. Prick dough with a fork in several areas. Bake at 375 degrees for 25 minutes or until golden brown.

Final Assembly of Hemisphere

Ingredients:
2 cups sliced sugared strawberries sprinkled with Grand Marnier
Flan pastry crust

(ingredients continued on next page)

Raspberry mousse molded in a 2½-quart mixing bowl

2 cups heavy cream whipped to stiff peaks with ⅓ cup confectioners' sugar and 1 teaspoon vanilla extract

6 strawberries cut into quarters

1 whole strawberry

1 lime

Method:

1. Place the sliced sweetened strawberries in bottom of pastry crust.
2. Unmold raspberry mousse on top of strawberries by first unmolding on an oiled cookie sheet and then sliding mousse onto strawberries.
3. Using a pastry bag and star tube (see Working with a Pastry Bag, page 204), pipe out double rosettes along the bottom of the mousse and crust. Place a quartered strawberry on each double rosette. Decorate top of mousse with whipped cream. Top with whole strawberry and thin slices of lime.

Menu
27

Sparkling Water with Lime

Green Bean Salad Canapés

Veal Scaloppine Marsala with Mushrooms

Baked Zucchini Squash

Cherry Tomatoes with Fresh Basil

Kiwibluba Dessert
(kiwifruit, blueberries and bananas with whipped frozen yogurt)

Sparkling Water with Lime

No beverage can claim to be lighter than water. It has no calories, no saccharin, no artificial coloring or flavoring, no caffeine or alcohol. Water is simple; it's totally natural. After all, your body contains 63 percent water!

Ingredients:

1 quart chilled sparkling water

6 lime wedges

Method:

1. Fill chilled cocktail glasses with sparkling water and squeeze a wedge of lime into each glass.

Green Bean Salad Canapés

Ingredients:

Rye bread

1 tablespoon olive oil

1 large onion sliced

2 tablespoons dry sherry

¾ pound green beans, cooked

½ teaspoon salt

1/8 teaspoon pepper

Radicchio lettuce leaves

6 sprigs of parsley

Method:

1. Preheat oven to 400 degrees.
2. Cut out 18 rye bread rounds using a 2-inch round cutter. Bake rounds on a sheet pan in 400-degree oven 10-15 minutes until well toasted.
3. Heat oil in a large skillet. Sauté onions over high heat until onions show browning along the edges. Add sherry and cook until liquid is evaporated.
4. Pass the onions and green beans through a meat grinder or chop in a food processor. Season mixture with salt and pepper.
5. Scoop a 1-ounce portion of green bean mixture on rye rounds. Place

canapés evenly spaced on a platter. Decorate with Radicchio lettuce leaves and parsley for contrasting color.

Veal Scaloppine Marsala with Mushrooms

Ingredients:

2 pounds boned-out veal meat cut into ¼-inch slices against the grain

Salt and pepper

Olive oil

4 cups sliced mushrooms

2 cups strong veal stock (See recipe for Beef Stock, page 198. Substitute veal bones for beef bones.)

1 cup dry Marsala wine

1 tablespoon arrowroot or cornstarch blended with 2 tablespoons Marsala wine

1 tablespoon chopped parsley

A few thin slices of lemon

Method:

1. Dry veal scallops and season with salt and pepper.
2. Using a pastry brush, lightly coat a nonstick or well-seasoned skillet with olive oil. Saute the sliced mushrooms on high heat until crisp and brown on the outside. Set aside.
3. In the same skillet saute the veal scallops over high heat less than 20 seconds on each side. Scallops should be browned on the outside and have a slightly pink tinge in the center. Remove veal and keep warm with the mushrooms.
4. Add the veal stock and Marsala wine to skillet. Thicken with cornstarch mixture. Reduce sauce until it is thick enough to lightly coat a spoon. The sauce should not be too thick or lumpy. Add chopped parsley to sauce.
5. Arrange veal in the center of a serving platter with the mushrooms around the border. Pour sauce over veal and mushrooms and serve decorated with a few slices of lemon.

Baked Zucchini Squash

Ingredients:

3 medium zucchini squash

Oil seasoned with garlic (To keep seasoned garlic oil on hand, pour oil into a jar and add peeled cloves of garlic. Use when needed.)

Grated Parmesan cheese

Method:

1. Preheat oven to 450 degrees.

2. Wash zucchini and cut in half lengthwise. Cut a small slice from the bottom of each half of zucchini so that it will rest on a baking sheet without tilting over.

3. Place squash in a baking pan and brush a small amount of garlic oil on each piece. Sprinkle grated Parmesan cheese on top.

4. Add a little water in the bottom of the baking pan and bake in a 450-degree oven for 25-30 minutes until zucchini is tender but not limp. Cheese should be browned slightly on top; if not, zucchini may be placed under a broiler to desired brownness.

Cherry Tomatoes with Fresh Basil

Ingredients:

1 pint cherry tomatoes

1 tablespoon chopped, preferably fresh, basil

½ cup beef stock or beef consommé (see Stocks -- Les Fonds de Cuisine, page 197)

½ teaspoon sugar

Method:

1. In a skillet toss all of the ingredients together while cooking, un-covered, over high heat. Cook until the liquid is reduced to a syrupy consistency and the tomatoes are tender but still hold their shape.

Kiwibluba Dessert

Ingredients:

4 kiwifruit

2 bananas

2 pints blueberries (fresh or frozen)

4 cups frozen vanilla yogurt (see next recipe)

Method:

1. Peel kiwifruit and slice each one into 6 round pieces. Peel bananas, cut in half lengthwise and slice into 1½-inch pieces. Mound blue-berries in the center of a large oval or round platter. Intermingle the cut kiwifruit and bananas around the mound of blueberries.

2. Beat frozen yogurt in a mixing bowl until it has a soft consistency.

Pour into a chilled serving bowl and serve on the side with the prepared fruit platter.

Frozen Vanilla Yogurt

Ingredients:

5 egg yolks or 2 whole eggs

¾ cup light brown sugar

1 cup milk or 2% milk

3 cups yogurt

2 teaspoons vanilla extract

Method:

1. In a heavy metal saucepan over medium high heat beat the egg yolks, sugar and milk together with a wire whisk. Stirring constantly, bring mixture to 180 degrees, as measured by a rapid-reading thermometer. Remove from heat, beat in yogurt and vanilla extract.

2. Freeze in ice cream maker packed with 3 to 4 parts of ice to 1 part of rock salt. For best results, serve frozen yogurt as soon as it is made while it is thick and still creamy. If you wish to make the frozen yogurt beforehand and freeze it, soften the yogurt at room temperature and beat with a heavy wire whisk just before serving.

Menu 28

Coleslaw Salad

Baked Trout Stuffed with Crabmeat

Tomatoes Rachel

(baked tomatoes with wheat germ and Parmesan cheese)

Fresh Long-Stemmed Strawberries

★Oatmeal Raisin Nut Cookies

Coleslaw Salad

Ingredients:

1 large head green cabbage (preferably a Savoy cabbage)

½ cup Yogurt Mayonnaise (see recipe on page 83) or
    regular mayonnaise

2 tablespoons wine vinegar

1 tablespoon honey

½ tablespoon poppyseeds

½ teaspoon salt

1/8 teaspoon black pepper

Beds of Boston lettuce or large outer leaves from the Savoy cabbage

1 tablespoon finely diced green bell pepper

1 tablespoon finely diced red bell pepper

1 tablespoon finely diced truffle or black olives

Method:

1. Shred cabbage.
2. In a large bowl mix mayonnaise, vinegar, honey, poppyseeds, salt and pepper together. Add shredded cabbage and toss.
3. Serve coleslaw mounded on beds of Boston lettuce or cabbage leaves. Sprinkle with green pepper, red pepper and truffles.

Baked Trout Stuffed with Crabmeat

Ingredients:

2 tablespoons olive oil

2 cloves minced garlic

1 cup chopped mushrooms

8 ounces crabmeat

1 teaspoon chopped parsley

2 tablespoons dry sherry

Salt and pepper to taste

(ingredients continued on next page)

6 5-ounce boneless trout

Melted butter

Lemon juice

Bread crumbs

Method:

1. Preheat oven to 400 degrees.

2. Heat oil in fry pan. Sauté garlic in oil for about a minute, watching to make sure garlic does not burn. Add mushrooms, crabmeat, parsley and sherry. Cook until most of the moisture is evaporated. Season to taste with salt and pepper. Set aside.

3. Remove top and side fins from trout. Heads and tails may be left on or removed depending on one's preference. Stuff each trout with crabmeat mixture.

4. Place fish on nonstick or lightly oiled baking pan. Brush lightly with butter. Sprinkle with lemon juice and bread crumbs. Bake in a 400-degree oven for 20 to 25 minutes.

Tomatoes Rachel

Ingredients:

3 large ripe tomatoes

4½ tablespoons Parmesan cheese

2½ tablespoons wheat germ

Method:

1. Preheat oven to 450 degrees.

2. Remove top stems from tomatoes. Cut tomatoes in half horizontally. Gently remove seeds with a teaspoon. Place tomato halves on a nonstick or lightly oiled baking pan, cut side up.

3. Mix Parmesan cheese and wheat germ together. Spinkle 1 tablespoon cheese mixture on top of each tomato.

4. Bake in 450-degree oven for 10 to 15 minutes until tomatoes feel soft to the touch and the cheese mixture is lightly browned. If necessary, place tomatoes under a broiler to achieve proper browning without overbaking tomato.

5. Tomatoes and trout may be arranged attractively together on a large platter decorated with fresh herbs and lemon wedges. This will make for an interesting color and shape combination.

Fresh Long-Stemmed Strawberries

During the months of April, May and June when California straw-berries are at their peak season, and when the weather and other conditions have been favorable for a good harvest, one can find the "crown jewel" of the berries -- the long-stemmed strawberry. These are large, sweet, red berries weighing around two ounces each, with a long stem left intact. They are a marvelous treat. My advice is: When you can find them -- serve them!

Ingredients:

3 pints strawberries (preferably long-stemmed)

Method:

1. Wash berries and trim stems to 1½ inches. Serve on a large platter.

★ Oatmeal Raisin Nut Cookies
(makes 4 dozen cookies; freeze well)

Ingredients:

6 ounces unsalted butter

1 cup brown sugar

1 egg

2 tablespoons water

1 teaspoon vanilla extract

3 cups oats

1 cup whole-wheat flour

1 teaspoon salt

½ teaspoon baking soda

1 cup slivered almonds

1 cup pecans

½ cup chopped raisins

Method:

1. Preheat oven to 375 degrees.
2. Cream butter and sugar together in a mixing bowl. Add the egg, water, vanilla and oats.

3. Sift the flour with the salt and baking soda. Add to mixture. Add nuts and raisins.

4. Using a small scoop or a large spoon, portion out dough on lightly greased or nonstick baking pans.

5. Bake in 375-degree oven for about 15 minutes.

Menu 29

Saffron Soup with Red Pepper and Spinach

Barbecued Rock Cornish Game Hens

Celery, Peas and Smokehouse Almonds

Baked Coriander Carrots

★ Brandy Cranapple Flan

Saffron Soup with Red Peppers and Spinach

Ingredients:

¼ teaspoon whole saffron

2 quarts strongly flavored chicken stock or canned chicken consommé (see Stocks -- Les Fonds de Cuisine, page 197)

1 large red bell pepper cut into 18 one-inch diamonds

2 cup fresh spinach leaves

2 tablespoons dry sherry

Method:

1. Simmer saffron in chicken stock for about 20 minutes. Strain out saffron threads and discard.

2. Add red pepper to soup and cook until tender; strain out and set aside.

3. Before serving, place 3 red pepper diamonds and a few spinach leaves into each soup bowl. Add sherry to hot chicken broth, pour into soup bowls and serve.

Barbecued Rock Cornish Game Hens

Ingredients:

½ cup soy sauce

¼ cup honey

¼ cup apricot preserves

¼ cup chili sauce

½ teaspoon Coleman's mustard or other hot powdered mustard

3 24-ounce Cornish hens

Method:

1. Mix the first 5 ingredients together to make barbecue sauce. Cut hens in half and marinate in sauce for at least 3 hours.

2. To cook in oven: Place hens on a lightly oiled or nonstick baking pan skin side up and bake in a preheated 375-degree oven for about 50 minutes, until there is just a trace of pink left along the thigh bone. (This can be checked by making a small incision with a paring knife.) Baste hens with barbecue sauce and place under a preheated broiler for a few minutes for final browning.

   To cook on a charcoal broiler: Place hens skin side up on a grid over a uniform bed of hot charcoal. Cook for about 10 minutes, turn birds skin side down. Continue cooking until there is just a trace of pink left along the thigh bone. Baste hens with barbecue sauce, cook a few more minutes while turning over until crisp and brown.

Celery, Peas and Smokehouse Almonds

Ingredients:

4 cups diced celery

1½ cups strong-flavored chicken stock or canned chicken consommé
 (see Stocks -- Les Fonds de Cuisine, page 197)

2 cups frozen peas

⅓ cup smokehouse almonds

Fresh sprigs of mint

Method:

1. In a covered saucepan, cook celery in chicken stock until tender but still crunchy. Remove from heat, let cool then refrigerate celery in stock overnight.
2. Before serving, reheat celery in stock, add peas, toss and heat. Strain out liquid, place celery and peas on a platter and garnish top with almonds and sides of platter with sprigs of mint.

Baked Coriander Carrots

Ingredients:

2 pounds carrots

1 tablespoon melted butter

¼ cup whole-wheat bread crumbs mixed with 1 teaspoon ground coriander

Method:

1. Preheat oven to 400 degrees.
2. Peel and cut carrots into 3-inch long and ½-inch wide pieces. Toss pieces in butter and then into bread crumb mixture.
3. Lay out carrots on a lightly greased or nonstick baking pan. Bake at 400 degrees until tender, for about 45 minutes.

★ Brandy Cranapple Flan

Ingredients:

Flan crust (see recipe on page 123)

8 large baking apples

1 cup fresh or frozen cranberries

(ingredients continued on next page)

3 tablespoons apricot preserves

1 pint apple juice

¼ cup brandy

2 teaspoons granulated sugar

½ cup apricot preserves strained through a sieve

¼ cup chopped unsalted, uncolored pistachio nuts or chopped
toasted almonds

Method:

1. Preheat oven to 375 degrees.

2. Make flan crust according to recipe.

3. Peel 6 apples, remove core and cut into small chunks. Place the apples in a heavy metal saucepan. Add the cranberries, apricot preserves, apple juice and brandy. Cook over high heat until apple mixture is thick and can hold its shape when mounded. Spread mixture into baked pastry shell.

4. Cut remaining 2 apples in half. Peel and core them. Cut apple halves into 1/8-to ¼-inch slices. Cover cranapple sauce mixture with a neat, closely overlapping layer of sliced apples arranged in a spiral. Sprinkle with granulated sugar. Bake in 375-degree oven for 20 minutes. Allow flan to cool before removing from mold.

5. Heat strained apricot preserves in a saucepan and brush on entire flan including crust. Place chopped pistachio nuts or toasted almonds around crust.

Menu
30

Michael's Jicama Hors d'oeuvres

Roast Loin of Pork with Sliced Apples

Steamed Honeyed Carrots and Parsnips

Swiss Chard

Melon with Prunes

★Animal Cracker Cookies

Michael's Jicama Hors d'oeuvres

Visitors to Mexico will see wandering vendors carrying platters of sliced jicama (pronounced hick-a-ma) seasoned with salt and a bit of Mexican parsley or cilantro. Jicama is somewhat juicy, has a mild, sweet flavor and has crunchiness similar to a water chestnut; most often served raw, it may also be boiled, steamed or fried.

Ingredients:

1 8-ounce package Neufchatel cheese or cream cheese at room temperature

1½ tablespoons minced green chile peppers

1 minced clove of garlic

½ teaspoon salt

1/8 teaspoon paprika

1 large jicama (carrots or turnips may be used if jicama is not available)

1 red or green pepper

Fresh flower

Parsley sprigs

Method:

1. Mix the cheese, chile peppers, garlic, salt and paprika together until a smooth paste has formed.
2. With a sharp knife, cut the jicama into julienne pieces approximately 2 inches long, ¾ inches wide and ½ inch in thickness. Take care so that all of the pieces are cut uniformly.
3. Using a pastry bag with a No. 4 star tube (see Working with a Pastry Bag, page 204), pipe out 3 small rosettes on each piece of jicama. Decorate center rosette of each jicama with a small diamond cut from the green or red pepper. A small pimiento rose with leaves cut from green onions is another attractive decoration for the center rosette.
4. Lay out hors d'oeuvres on round platter in a formation resembling the spokes of a wheel. Place the flower in center of platter and garnish with parsley sprigs.

Roast Loin of Pork with Sliced Apples

Ingredients:

4½ lbs. boneless loin of pork

½ teaspoon rosemary

(ingredients continued on next page)

½ teaspoon dill weed

½ teaspoon thyme

½ teaspoon basil

1 teaspoon minced garlic

1 tablespoon olive oil

1 carrot finely chopped

1 onion finely chopped

1 stalk celery finely chopped

3 cups beef stock or beef consommé (see Stocks -- Les Fonds de Cuisine, page 197)

Prepared apples (see next recipe)

Sprigs of watercress

Method:

1. Trim off all visible signs of fat from loin.
2. At least 3 hours before roasting or preferably the day before roasting, rub the loin of pork with the oil, herbs and garlic.
3. Preheat oven to 350 degrees.
4. Place prepared pork loin in roasting pan and sprinkle chopped vegetables over it. Roast at 350 degrees for approximately 50 minutes until the internal temperature measures 160 degrees. When done, remove meat from pan and cover with aluminum foil to keep warm.
5. Add stock or consommé to vegetables in pan. Place pan over burner and scrape all the brown bits sticking to the bottom of the pan. Transfer vegetables and liquid to a saucepan, bring to a boil and cook until the juice has a good strong flavor. Discard vegetables, season to taste with salt and pepper. Keep warm.
6. After the pork has had a chance to rest for at least 15 minutes, cut ¼-inch slices and lay out neatly on a serving platter. Place a circle of sliced apples (see next recipe) around the meat. Garnish platter with watercress.

Ingredients for apple slices:

2 large Red Delicious apples

Butter

Allspice

Method:

1. Cut apples in half. Remove core and cut into ¼-inch slices. Lay slices out on a lightly buttered baking pan. Spinkle apples lightly with allspice. Bake in 350-degree oven for 25 minutes. (Apples may be baked in the same oven while roasting loin of pork.)

Pork Sauce

Ingredients:

½ cup apricot preserves

¼ cup Dijon mustard

¼ cup soy sauce

½ cup water

1 teaspoon Kitchen Bouquet (Sold in gourmet stores and most supermarkets. Kitchen Bouquet is excellent for adding a darker and richer color to soups and sauces.)

Method:

1. Purée all of the ingredients in a blender. Serve in a pitcher or in a sauceboat at room temperature.

Steamed Honeyed Carrots and Parsnips

Ingredients:

¾ pound medium carrots

¾ pound medium parsnips

2 teaspoons honey

2 teaspoons butter

2 cups water

Method:

1. Peel carrots and parsnips. Cut vegetables at an angle to produce uniform oval slices around ¼ inch in thickness.

2. Place the carrots in a skillet with a tight-fitting cover and add half of the honey, half of the butter and half of the water. Cover the skillet and cook on a medium heat for about 10 to 15 minutes until the carrots are tender but still slightly crunchy. Remove carrots and reduce liquid (if necessary) to a syrupy glaze. Pour glaze over carrots and set aside.

3. In the same skillet, repeat step 2 using the parsnips. Parsnips will generally take less time to cook than carrots. It is for this reason they are cooked separately.

4. Mix carrots into parsnips. Heat well before serving.

Swiss Chard

It's too bad Popeye didn't know that besides spinach, Swiss chard and many other dark green leafy vegetables serve as an excellent nutritional substitute. Just think, Popeye could have had a larger variety of food with which to energize, hence he and his sweetheart Olive Oyl could have lived in heavenly matrimony without his bizarre obsession for "me spinach."

Ingredients:

2 heads Swiss chard

2 teaspoons lemon juice or wine vinegar

Salt and pepper to taste

Method:

1. Wash leaves very thoroughly to remove all sand and soil. Trim any tough stems. Cut in large pieces and put in a saucepan with a small amount of boiling water.

2. Cover and steam for 10 to 12 minutes, or just until chard is tender. Take care not to overcook.

3. Remove from heat, add lemon juice or wine vinegar and season to taste with salt and pepper.

Melon with Prunes

Melon is somewhat like a book, in that you can't always tell its contents by its cover. As a result, the surest way to tell if a melon is sweet and juicy is to taste it. This may not always be possible, especially when buying just one melon.

As a general guide to selection of all melons, the outer skin should be a good color and give off a rich aroma. The melon should feel heavy for its size, and yield slightly when pressed with the thumbs at the blossom end. A slight rattling of the seeds, when shaken, is a sign of maturity; however, loose, watery seeds are, more likely, the first sign of the last stages of maturity and it could be slightly sour; or, it might be the finest melon you've ever tasted!

Ingredients:

1 fully ripened cantaloupe melon or other orange-fleshed melon

1 fully ripened honeydew melon or other green-fleshed melon

12 cooked prunes

1 lemon

1 lime

A few sprigs of fresh mint, if available

Method:

1. Cut melons in half and remove seeds. Cut into 2-inch slices; remove rind and cut melon slices into 2-inch pieces. Intermingle honeydew and cantaloupe pieces on a large platter. Place the prunes on top.

2. Cut a few thin round slices of lemon and lime. Make a radius cut into each slice, twist and stand on two ends forming lemon and lime curls. Garnish melon platter at various intervals with curls. Squeeze juice from remaining lemon and lime over the melon and prunes.

3. Place a few sprigs of mint around platter and serve.

★Animal Cracker Cookies

Ingredients:

¼ pound softened unsalted butter

⅓ cup brown sugar

1 egg

¼ cup finely ground pecans (use a food processor or meat grinder)

½ teaspoon salt

½ tablespoon vanilla extract

½ cup whole-wheat flour

1 cup unbleached all-purpose flour

Confectioners' sugar

Method:

1. In a mixing bowl cream butter and sugar. Add egg, pecans, salt and vanilla. Sift flours together and fold into batter. Refrigerate dough for at least ½ hour.

2. Roll out dough on wax paper to ¼ inch in thickness. Cut out shapes with small animal cutters. (Cutters are available in sets that can be purchased in most gourmet stores or restaurant supply stores.) Place on nonstick or lightly greased sheet pans. Bake in a preheated oven at 375 degrees for 10 to 12 minutes.

3. Before serving spinkle lightly with confectioners' sugar.

Menu
31

Iced Red Zinger Tea

Caesar Salad with Pine Nuts

Brady Boy's Baked Eggplant Parmesan

★ Sandy's Cheesecake

Iced Red Zinger Tea

Ingredients:
8 bags of Red Zinger tea
3 quarts water
Lemon wedges

Method:
1. Add tea bags to water and refrigerate for at least 2 hours. Stir, remove tea bags and serve in tall glasses over ice with lemon wedges.

Caesar Salad with Pine Nuts

According to the International Society of Epicures in Paris, Caesar Salad is the greatest original dish to come out of the United States in the past fifty years.

Caesar Cardini created the salad by circumstances. It was the Fourth of July weekend more than forty years ago. His restaurant was just about out of food and the suppliers were closed. He went back to the kitchen to take inventory and found a few crates of romaine lettuce, half a crate of eggs and some stale bread. He rubbed a bowl with garlic, broke up the romaine lettuce and coddled the eggs. Then the stale bread was cut up and soaked in olive oil and put in the oven to toast. The eggs were mixed with the lettuce, pear vinegar and green olive oil. Grated cheese and toasted croutons were added to this. He decided to dramatize the salad since it was a one-dish item. So he called his waiters and instructed them to mix it on the serving cart next to the customer's table. It was a success!

Ingredients:
3 slices of whole-wheat bread cut into cubes
2 heads of romaine lettuce
2 tablespoons olive oil
4 tablespoons chicken consommé (see Stocks -- Les Fonds de Cuisine, page 197)
4 tablespoons red wine vinegar
2 coddled eggs (cooked for 1½ minutes in simering water)
1 large clove minced garlic
½ cup Parmesan cheese
5 anchovy filets minced
Pinch of dry mustard
¼ cup pine nuts
Salt and pepper to taste

Coleslaw Salad (page 131); Mama Es' Salad (page 175);
Broccoli, Beets and Chick Pea Salad (page 155)

Cranapple Nedlogs (page 21)

The Black Mirror Cake (page 84)

Three Cheese Omelet and High-Fiber Bran Muffins (page 24)

Sautéed Bay Scallops (page 119)

Amaretto Buttermilk Pancakes (page 28)

Sandy's Cheesecake (page 148)

Ensalada Mexicano with Chilled Hibiscus Tea (page 46)

Veal and Vegetable Decoupage (page 60)

Strawberry Raspberry Hemisphere (page 122)

Botanical Fruit (page 24)

Baked Filet of Sole with Spinach Boats and
Steamed Banana Squash (page 186)

Fried Pastries with Cinnamon and Lemon Mist Tea (page 173)

Cheese Soufflé (page 72)

Lobster Tails Fra Diavolo (page 112)

Gingered Duck Salad (page 97)

Crabmeat Lahvosh (page 43)

Eight Seasons Chicken Salad in Pita Bread
with Orange and Almond Salad (page 54)

Roast Duck with Blackberry Orange Sauce (page 181)

Brandy Cranapple Flan (page 137)

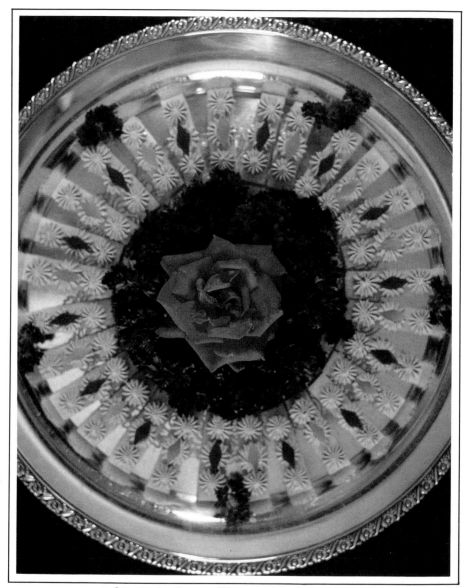

Michael's Jicama Hors d'oeuvres (page 140)

Initialed Consommé (page 91)

Poached Chicken Breasts Dolphin (page 107)

Raspberry Ice (page 61)

Method:

1. Bake bread cubes in 400-degree oven for 10 minutes until golden brown.
2. Wash romaine, drain and dry; break into bite-size pieces.
3. In a salad bowl, add all of the ingredients (except croutons) and toss mixture gently until no trace of egg is to be seen.
4. Taste for seasoning.
5. Before serving, garnish with croutons.

Brady Boy's Baked Eggplant Parmesan

This dish has been on the Maine Chance menu for nine years; there's still no sign that the guests are ready for a change.

Ingredients:

1 large or two small eggplant
1 egg beaten with ¼ cup milk
¾ cup whole-wheat bread crumbs
3 cups Marinara Sauce (see next recipe)
1 pint ricotta cheese
6 slices mozzarella cheese, ¼ inch thick
Grated Parmesan cheese
2 pounds cooked broccoli (see About Cooking Vegetables, page 200)
1 pint large mushrooms sliced and quickly stir-fried in a nonstick frypan

Method:

1. Preheat oven to 400 degrees.
2. Peel and slice eggplant 1 inch in thickness and about 3½ inches in diameter.
3. Dip eggplant into egg mixture, then into bread crumbs.
4. Place eggplant on a baking sheet and bake in oven at 400 degrees for about 25 to 30 minutes or until eggplant is just tender.
5. Preheat oven to 500 degrees.
6. Place the eggplant in a large casserole or in individual casseroles. Pour ½ cup Marinara Sauce over each piece. Place a small scoop of ricotta cheese in center and top with a slice of mozzarella cheese. Sprinkle lightly with Parmesan cheese. Place broccoli and mushrooms around eggplant.
7. When ready to serve, place the prepared eggplant in the 500-degree oven for about 15 minutes. Bake until the cheese is melted and begins to turn brown.

Marinara Sauce

Ingredients:

1 tablespoon olive oil

1 small onion finely chopped

1 teaspoon chopped garlic

6 large tomatoes peeled and coarsely chopped (for easy peeling, plunge
tomatoes into boiling water for 10 seconds)
or 1 28-ounce can peeled crushed tomatoes

1 cup tomato paste

2 teaspoons fresh chopped oregano or 1 teaspoon dried

2 teaspoons fresh chopped basil or 1 teaspoon dried

1 teaspoon salt

1/8 teaspoon crushed red pepper

Method:

1. Heat the oil in a saucepan and cook the onion until soft and transparent.

2. Add the garlic and cook for another minute.

3. Add the remaining ingredients and simmer for about 20 to 30 minutes until the sauce has thickened.

Sandy's Cheesecake
(serves 12 people)

Ingredients:

2½ cups graham cracker crumbs

½ cup melted unsalted butter

1½ cups heavy cream

18 ounces cream cheese

1⅓ cups confectioners' sugar

2 teaspoons pure vanilla extract

¼ cup yogurt or sour cream

Fresh berries

Method:

1. Preheat oven to 400 degrees.

2. Combine the graham cracker crumbs and melted butter.

3. Place graham cracker mixture in an 11-inch flan mold with a removable bottom. Working with your hands form a crust with a 1-inch ridge along the perimeter. Bake crust at 400 degrees for 10 minutes.

4. In a chilled bowl whip the heavy cream until stiff peaks are formed; refrigerate.

5. Cream the cheese and confectioners' sugar together until well blended with no signs of lumps. Add the vanilla extract.

6. Fold the whipped cream into the cream cheese mixture and distribute two-thirds of the mixture into the graham cracker crust. Smooth out with spatula and spread top with yogurt or sour cream.

7. Using a pastry bag and star tube (see Working with a Pastry Bag, page 204), pipe out rosettes along perimeter of cake with the remaining cream cheese mixture.

8. Garnish rosettes with fresh berries and refrigerate at least 2 hours before serving.

Menu
32

Chiffonade Salad
*(tossed greens with hard-boiled egg, julienne beets
and chopped chives)*

Coq au Vin
(chicken simmered in red wine sauce)

Wild and Brown Rice

Asparagus

Blackberry Coupe

Chiffonade Salad

Ingredients:

12 cups mixed greens (see About Preparing Salad Greens, page 202)

French Dressing (see recipe on page 64)

1 chopped hard-boiled egg

½ cup cooked julienne beets

2 tablespoons fresh cut chives or frozen cut chives

Method:

1. Toss salad greens with dressing. Arrange greens in a large chilled salad bowl or in individual chilled salad plates. Garnish top of greens with egg, beets an chives.

Coq au Vin

Coq au Vin or chicken in wine, a French classic, is made with either red or white wine. I prefer using red wine which gives the dish more character. Try making this dish the day before you plan to serve it so the chicken has a chance to absorb the flavor of the sauce. It's one of those dishes, like most stews, the day after tastes better than the day before.

Ingredients:

Oil

12 peeled white boiling onions

2 2½- to 3-pound fryers cut into quarters

Salt and pepper

3 cups red wine

3 cups beef stock or beef consommé (see Stocks -- Les Fonds de Cuisine, page 197)

¼ cup cognac

2 cloves minced garlic

¼ teaspoon thyme

1 bay leaf

2 slices very crisp bacon, chopped

2 tablespoons cornstarch mixed with ¼ cup red wine

1 tablespoon clarified butter

10 large sliced mushrooms

Chopped parsley

1 bunch watercress

Method:

1. Preheat oven broiler.

2. In a roasting pan rub a little oil over onions and brown under broiler. Remove from pan and set aside. Dry off chicken, rub with oil, salt and pepper, place in roasting pan and brown on both sides under broiler.

3. In a pot heat the wine, stock and cognac. Add garlic, thyme, bay leaf and bacon. Add onions to pot, cook for about 20 minutes until tender. Remove onions and set aside. Add chicken to pot and simmer for about 40 minutes until chicken is tender and the juices run yellow. Remove chicken and set aside.

4. Skim fat off of liquid and thicken with cornstarch/wine mixture. Reduce sauce until it is thick enough to lightly coat a spoon.

5. Add butter to skillet and sauté mushrooms over high heat.

6. Before serving reheat chicken and onions in sauce, arrange chicken on a platter, breasts on one side, legs on the other, place onions and mushrooms over chicken, baste with sauce and sprinkle with chopped parsley. Garnish center of platter with watercress sprigs.

Wild and Brown Rice

Wild and brown rice make a nice couple. They take the same time to cook. They're both complex carbohydrates (natural foods) and they certainly look good together.

Ingredients:

4 cups strong-tasting chicken stock or canned chicken consommé
(see Stocks -- Les Fonds de Cuisine, page 197)

1 cup long grain brown rice

1 cup wild rice

Method:

1. In a skillet bring the stock or consommé to a boil. Rinse rice with cold water and drain well. Add rice, cover and cook over low heat for approximately 50 minutes until rice is tender but not mushy.

Asparagus

Ingredients:

2 pounds asparagus

Method:

1. If the asparagus is not absolutely young, it is best to peel the stalks thinly with a paring knife and remove the ends that are tough. Trim the asparagus so that they are all the same length. Wash and tie the asparagus in a bunch.

2. Bring a large pot of water to a boil. Add asparagus, adjust heat so that the water continues to simmer. Cook the asparagus for approximately 15 minutes. The stalks should still be crunchy but cooked enough so that a fork could cut through them.

3. When done, remove the asparagus from water, cut string, and lay out asparagus on a tilted flat pan so that they may drain while cooling. To serve, lay out asparagus in neetly formed rows on one side and a mound of rice mixture on the other side of an oval serving platter. Cover with aluminum foil, place in a 250-degree oven for about 15 minutes until heated through. Remove foil and serve.

Blackberry Coupe

Ingredients:

6 ounces sour cream or yogurt

6 ripe peeled peach or pear halves (substitute canned fruit if fresh fruit is not available)

2 cups fresh, frozen or canned blackberries

Honey

Method:

1. Place a 1-ounce scoop of sour cream or yogurt in a champagne glass (flat round style) and top with a peach or pear half.

2. Purée the blackberries in a blender for a few minutes until a thick smooth puree is formed. Strain out the seeds and, if necessary, add honey for more sweetness. Pour puree on top of each peach or pear and serve.

Menu
33

Cranberry Apple Juice

Broccoli, Beets and Chick-Pea Salad

Baked Acorn Squash with Turkey
and Wild Rice Stuffing

★ Zucchini Cake
with Cream Cheese Raisin Frosting

Cranberry Apple Juice

Ingredients:

12 ounces cranberry juice

12 ounces unfiltered apple juice

Method:

1. Mix together and serve in chilled cocktail glasses.

Broccoli, Beets and Chick-Pea Salad

Ingredients:

2 pounds cooked broccoli cut into sprigs (see About Cooking Vegetables, page 200)

2 cups peeled and cooked baby beets or one 16-ounce can of small whole beets

¾ cup canned or cooked garbanzo beans (chick peas)

1½ cups Arden Dressing (see recipe on page 94)

Method:

1. Lay out broccoli sprigs with stems down on a large platter or individual salad plates. Stud with beets and sprinkle with garbanzo beans. Spoon Arden Dressing across top and serve. Salad tastes good chilled or at room temperature.

Baked Acorn Squash with Turkey and Wild Rice Stuffing

Ingredients:

3 1½-pound acorn squash

2 cups full-flavored turkey stock or canned chicken consommé (see Stocks -- Les Fonds de Cuisine, page 197)

½ cup brown rice

½ cup wild rice

½ cup chopped celery

½ cup chopped onion

2 tablespoons walnut or olive oil

2 cups diced cooked turkey or chicken

(ingredients continued on next page)

¼ cup dry sherry or brandy

1 teaspoon rosemary

1 teaspoon chopped sage

2 tablespoons chopped parsley

¼ cup slivered toasted almonds (toast almonds in 400-degree oven for about 10 minutes)

Salt and pepper to taste

Large red cabbage leaves

Fresh herb sprigs (parsley, sage, rosemary)

Method:

1. Poke a few holes into acorn squash, place on a baking pan and bake in a 400-degree oven for 1 hour and 15 minutes until tender to the touch; slice in half and remove seeds.

2. Add stock, brown rice and wild rice to a saucepan, cover and cook on a low heat for about 50 minutes until rice has absorbed all the liquid.

3. In a large skillet, sauté the celery and onion in oil until onion is translucent and slightly browned. Remove from heat, add rice, turkey, sherry, herbs and almonds. Mix and season to taste with salt and pepper.

4. Portion out mixture into the cavity of each acorn squash. Before serving, heat squash in a covered casserole; remove from casserole and serve on a large platter or individual dinner plates lined with a bed of red cabbage leaves and garnished with fresh herbs.

★ Zucchini Cake
with Cream Cheese Raisin Frosting

Ingredients:

3 eggs

2 cups granulated sugar

1 cup safflower oil

½ tablespoon vanilla extract

2 cups grated unpeeled zucchini

1 cup chopped pecans

3 cups unsifted whole-wheat flour

½ teaspoon baking powder

(ingredients continued on next page)

1 teaspoon baking soda

1 teaspoon salt

1 tablespoon cinnamon

1 teaspoon nutmeg

1 teaspoon allspice

8 ounces cream cheese at room temperature

¼ cup chopped golden raisins

Confectioners' sugar to sprinkle on top of cake

Method:

1. Preheat oven to 350 degrees.

2. In a mixing bowl, beat eggs on high speed until foamy. Add sugar gradually until mixture is thick and holds its shape for a moment as it falls from the uplifted arm of the beater into the mixing bowl. Add oil and vanilla extract slowly while still beating. Stir in the grated zucchini and chopped pecans.

3. In a separate bowl, mix the remaining dry ingredients together until well blended. Add the flour mixture to egg mixture. Mix on low speed just until well blended.

4. Pour mixture into a nonstick or a greased and floured 10-inch cake pan or a loaf pan. Bake for 1 hour and 15 minutes at 350 degrees. Let cool before frosting.

5. Mix cream cheese and raisins until well blended. Cut the top third of the zucchini cake off and break into crumbs. Ice top of remaining cake with frosting. Gather crumbs and place on top of frosting. Sprinkle lightly with confectioners' sugar.

Menu
34

Sparkling Cider

Crabmeat Artichoke Hors d'oeuvres

Broiled Filet of Beef Teriyaki

**Oriental Style Broccoli
with Red Pepper and Cashew Nuts**

Brown Rice with Scallions

The New Dessert
(yogurt with melon balls, Bing cherries and honey)

Sparkling Cider

For a delicious, nonalcoholic drink that can be used for toasting and celebrating special occasions, to take the place of champagne, I suggest serving sparkling cider. Stephen Martinelli may be considered the Dom Perignon of apple cider. He and his family have been bottling his award-winning apple juice products in California for more than one hundred and ten years. I have found no equal to their sparkling cider.

Ingredients:

2 fifths chilled Martinelli's sparkling cider

Method:

1. Fill chilled champagne glasses with sparkling cider and serve.

Crabmeat Artichoke Hors d'oeuvres

Ingredients:

12 freshly cooked or canned baby artichoke hearts

¼ pound finely chopped crabmeat

1 tablespoon chopped parsley

1/8 teaspoon Tabasco sauce

½ teaspoon lemon juice

¼ teaspoon garlic salt

3 tablespoons Yogurt Mayonnaise (see recipe on page 83) or regular mayonnaise

Apple bird and parsley sprigs for garnish

Method:

1. Cut a slice off of the bottom of each artichoke so it will stand upright. With your fingers, or with the back of a teaspoon, depress the center of each artichoke forming a cup. Place artichoke cups upside down on a towel to drain any excess liquid.

2. Mix the crabmeat salad ingredients together. Taste for seasoning. Stuff each artichoke cup with crabmeat salad.

3. To serve, arrange artichoke cups on a platter. Garnish center of platter with apple bird and parsley sprigs.

(diagram of apple bird on next page)

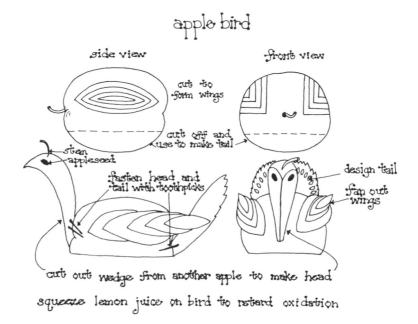

apple bird

side view   front view

cut to form wings

cut off and use to make tail

stem appleseed

design tail

fan out wings

fasten head and tail with toothpicks

cut out wedge from another apple to make head

squeeze lemon juice on bird to retard oxidation

The Very Tender Tenderloin

From the filet of beef or tenderloin we derive our Filet Mignon, Tournedos, Chateaubriand, Beef Stroganoff and the famous Beef Wellington. To choose one word that would describe this choicest cut of meat would be "tender."

The least-used muscles produce the most tender cuts of meat. The tenderloin is an inside muscle that runs along the lower back of the steer. If it were to be compared to the muscles of the human body, it would be right in the area where we tend to develop love handles.

Unfortunately, tenderness and flavor do not go hand in hand. It is the untender, most-used muscles from the leg, rump and shoulders that have the most flavor and in turn make delicious meat loaves, stews, casseroles and soup stocks, but terribly chewy roasts and steaks. Putting cost aside, the tenderloin would be a poor choice to make hamburgers and soup stocks as it would result in a flavorless product.

Because of its mild flavor the tenderloin, whether cut as a roast, into steaks or into a stew, goes well with and is generally accompanied by a flavorful sauce or marinade. A well-prepared cut of meat from the tenderloin with a flavorful sauce or marinade is truly in a class by itself.

Broiled Filet of Beef Teriyaki

Ingredients for marinade:

½ cup beef stock or canned beef consommé (see Stocks -- Les Fonds de Cuisine, page 197)

½ cup soy sauce

2 tablespoons honey

2 tablespoons lemon juice

1 teaspoon chopped ginger

3 cloves chopped garlic

Other ingredients:

4 pounds beef tenderloin filet

1 tablespoon peanut oil

3 cups fresh mung bean sprouts or Enoki (Snow Puff) mushrooms

3 cups watercress sprigs

Purple onion water lilly (see diagram)

Method:

1. Combine all of the ingredients for marinade. Trim off all excess fat and skin from the beef tenderloin and marinate beef for 3 hours giving beef one-third turn after each hour.

2. Prepare charcoal broiler or preheat oven broiler. Dry beef with a towel. Pour marinade in a saucepan to heat up later. Brush beef with peanut oil and cook over or under medium heat for about 10 to 15 minutes. Turn over and cook on other side for another 10 to 15 minutes. It is hard to say precisely how long it will take to cook the beef as much depends on the intensity of the heat, degree of doneness desired, and the thickness of the filet. Filet of beef is commonly served medium-rare. A medium-rare roast, when pressed with the fingers, will be soft to the touch with some resiliency; it will measure between 120 and 130 degrees on the meat thermometer; and, when cut, it will be completely pink in the center. When roast is done, let rest for at least 15 minutes before slicing.

3. Heat marinade. Cut filet into ½-inch slices and lay out on one side of a 12- to 14-inch heated oval platter. Place a mound of watercress and a mound of mung sprouts on the opposite side of the platter. Pour the hot teriyaki marinade over meat and mung sprouts. Garnish corner of platter (watercress side) with onion water lilly (see diagram) and serve.

(diagram of purple onion water lilly on next page)

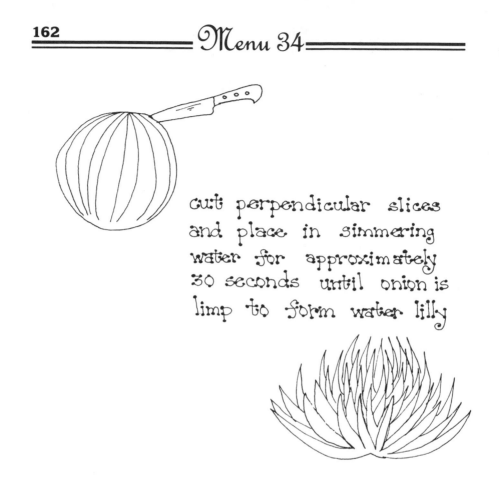

cut perpendicular slices
and place in simmering
water for approximately
30 seconds until onion is
limp to form water lily

Oriental Style Broccoli
with Red Pepper and Cashew Nuts

Ingredients:

2 pounds broccoli

1 large red bell pepper

1 cup beef stock or canned beef consommé (see Stocks -- Les Fonds de
   Cuisine, page 197)

¼ cup dry sherry

2 tablespoons cornstarch

¼ cup Kikkoman soy sauce

1 teaspoon finely minced ginger

1 teaspoon finely minced garlic

⅓ cup roasted unsalted cashew nuts (bake raw cashews in 400-degree
   oven for 20 minutes)

Method:

1. Wash broccoli and discard the coarse leaves. Separate the broccoli heads from the stems. Cut broccoli heads into 1½-inch pieces. Peel stems and cut into 1½-inch-long julienne pieces. Cut red pepper into 1½-inch-long julienne pieces.

2. Combine broccoli and beef stock in a skillet. Cover and steam for about 7 minutes, making sure broccoli is still crunchy with a bright green color. Remove broccoli and set aside. Add red pepper to skillet, cover and steam until tender but still crunchy. Remove red pepper and set aside.

3. Mix sherry with cornstarch until a smooth lump-free mixture is formed. Add cornstarch mixture, soy sauce, ginger and garlic to skillet. Stir and bring to a boil.

4. Before serving, toss and heat vegetables and cashew nuts in skillet with sauce.

Brown Rice with Scallions

Ingredients:

4 cups strong-flavored beef stock (see Stocks -- Les Fonds de Cuisine, page 197)

2 cups long grain brown rice

½ cup chopped scallions

Method:

1. Bring beef stock to a boil in a heavy metal saucepan with a tight-fitting cover. Rinse rice with cold water and drain well. Add rice, cover, reduce heat to low, and cook for 50 to 60 minutes until the rice is tender and has absorbed all of the liquid. Mix in scallions.

The New Dessert

Ingredients:

24 small melon balls scooped from a ripened honeydew or cantaloupe melon

24 canned or fresh pitted Bing cherries (if canned, drain well)

1½ cups plain yogurt

6 teaspoons warm honey

6 champagne glasses (flat round style)

Method:

1. Place a 2-ounce scoop of yogurt in the center of each champagne glass. Alternate 4 cherries with 4 melon balls around the rim of each glass.

2. Before serving, pour 1 teaspoon of warm honey over the yogurt in each champagne glass.

Menu
35

Papaya Apple Juice

Cucumbers in Yogurt Poppyseed Dressing

Bulgur Wheat Pilaf
with Skewered Vegetables

Fresh Strawberries with Hot Custard Sauce

Papaya Apple Juice

Ingredients:

1 quart unfiltered apple juice
1 ripe papaya peeled and seeded
1 tablespoon lime juice
6 thin slices of lime

Method:

1. Purée apple juice, papaya and lime juice in blender. Serve in chilled cocktail glasses garnished with a sliver of lime.

Cucumbers in Yogurt Poppyseed Dressing

Ingredients:

3 medium size cucumbers
1 cup plain yogurt
½ cup buttermilk
1 tablespoon plus 1 teaspoon honey
1/8 teaspoon black pepper
2 teaspoons poppyseeds

Method:

1. Clean and score rind of cucumber with the prongs of a fork. Cut cucumbers into less than ¼-inch-thick round slices.
2. Mix the remaining ingredients together in a bowl with a wire whip to make yogurt poppyseed dressing.
3. Toss cucumbers in dressing and serve on a chilled, colorful china platter.

Bulgur Wheat Pilaf with Skewered Vegetables

Ingredients for Bulgur Wheat Pilaf:

1 cup chopped onions
2 tablespoons safflower oil
1½ cups bulgur wheat (may be purchased in most health food stores)
3 cups water
⅓ cup dark raisins
⅓ cup golden raisins

(ingredients continued on next page)

½ cup shelled, unsalted, uncolored pistachio nuts

1 teaspoon cinnamon

½ teaspoon cayenne pepper

1 teaspoon salt

Method:

1. In a skillet with a tight-fitting cover saute the onions in the oil until soft and translucent.

2. Add bulgur wheat, stir and cook until golden.

3. Stir in remaining ingredients. Cover, bring to a boil, reduce heat and simmer for 15 minutes until all the water is absorbed and the bulgur wheat is tender but still crunchy.

One can dream up any combination of vegetables to put on the skewers. To give it the gourmet touch always try to vary shapes, colors and textures. Here is just one example:

Ingredients for Skewered Vegetables:

12 large mushroom caps

12 squares of cut red pepper about 2 inches by 2 inches

12 cauliflower buds about 2 inches in diameter

6 pieces of cut zucchini about 3 inches long

2 tablespoons honey

2 tablespoons melted butter

½ tablespoon lemon juice

½ cup cornmeal

1 teaspoon salt

Method:

1. Cook vegetables until tender but somewhat crunchy (see About Cooking Vegetables, page 200). On 6 skewers thread the vegetables in the following order: a mushroom cap, a red pepper square, a cauliflower bud, a piece of zucchini, a cauliflower bud, a red pepper square and a mushroom cap. Place skewered vegetables on a lightly greased or nonstick baking pan.

2. Mix honey, butter and lemon juice together and brush on vegetables.

3. Mix cornmeal and salt together. Sprinkle over vegetables.

4. Place prepared vegetables under a pre-heated broiler and broil until crumb topping is golden brown. Place over Bulgur Wheat Pilaf and serve.

Fresh Strawberries with Hot Custard Sauce

Ingredients:

2 cups milk

¼ cup sugar

2 tablespoons cornstarch

2 egg yolks

1 teaspoon pure vanilla extract

1 teaspoon brandy

2 pints fresh cleaned strawberries with stems removed

Method:

1. In a saucepan that is not made of aluminum, mix the milk, sugar, cornstarch and egg yolks thoroughly together until all lumps are dissolved. Cook over medium high heat, stirring constantly, until the mixture comes to a boil and thickens.

2. Remove from heat. Add vanilla extract and brandy. Keep warm until serving time.

3. Place strawberries in a bowl or platter, making sure the cut end of the berries are facing downward for a more attractive appearance. Pour hot custard sauce over berries and serve.

Menu 36

Orange and Mung Sprout Salad

Baked Salmon Nut Croquettes

★Fried Pastries with Cinnamon

Lemon Mist Tea

Orange and Mung Sprout Salad

Ingredients for Orange Belvedere Dressing:

¼ cup safflower oil

¼ cup tarragon vinegar

⅓ cup chicken consommé (see Stocks -- Les Fonds de Cuisine, page 197)

⅓ cup orange juice

1 tablespoon chopped parsley

Pinch of dry mustard

1/8 teaspoon black pepper

1 teaspoon honey

Ingredients for salad:

12 cups mixed greens (see About Cooking Vegetables, page 200)

1½ cups orange segments (peel orange, cut out segments between membranes)

2 cups mung bean sprouts

Method:

1. Make dressing by mixing all of the ingredients together. Chill well.

2. Before serving, gently toss greens with dressing, orange segments and sprouts, reserving some segments and sprouts for garnishing the top of the salad bowl.

Baked Salmon Nut Croquettes
(makes 1 dozen)

Chefs get recipes from cooking schools attended;
> from books, magazines and cooks they've apprehended.

Inventing new dishes is always satisfying.

This one being quite neat,
> is from the box of Bulgur Wheat.

But, it is a new creation,
> because there is variation.

A vegetable sauce and an extra ingredient,
> have made it most expedient.

Ingredients:

2½ cups water

1¼ cups Bulgur Wheat

1 16-ounce can sockeye red salmon or preferably 1 pound cooked fresh king salmon.

⅓ cup toasted slivered almonds (toast almonds in 400-degree oven for 10 minutes)

½ cup salmon liquid plus milk

2 eggs

1 tablespoon lemon juice

2 tablespoons pickle relish

¼ cup finely chopped onion

¼ teaspoon dill weed

¼ teaspoon salt (use 1 teaspoon salt if fresh salmon is used)
¼ teaspoon pepper

Method:

1. Preheat oven to 425 degrees.
2. In a pot with a lid, bring water to a boil. Add bulgur wheat, stir, lower heat, cover and simmer for 15 minutes until wheat has absorbed all of the water.
3. Add remaining ingredients to cooked bulgur wheat. Mix well.
4. Using a No. 10 scoop, portion out croquettes on a nonstick or lightly greased baking pan. Bake at 425 degrees for approximately 20 to 25 minutes until croquettes are crisp on the outside but still moist inside.

Ingredients for vegetable sauce:

1½ cups clam broth

1½ cups milk

1 small onion peeled and chopped

2 stalks celery chopped

2 cups chopped carrots

¼ cup chopped fresh chives

6 lemon wedges

Method:

1. In a heavy metal saucepan mix the clam broth, milk, onion, celery and carrots. Cook until vegetables are tender. Purée mixture in blender until a thick, smooth sauce is obtained. If necessary, keep

sauce warm in a double boiler. Before serving, ladle ¼-cup sauce over each croquette, sprinkle with chopped chives and serve with a lemon wedge on the side. Salmon nut croquettes may be attractively served on a platter garnished with an orange flower basket in the center.

Orange Basket with Flowers

1. Cut off bottom of orange so that it may rest on a flat surface.

2. Using a stripper knife, score a circumference around the center of the orange and make decorative scores resembling basket weaving on the lower half of the orange.

3. With a paring knife, make 2 slices from the top of the orange down through the center to form the basket handles. Cut zigzag edges around the orange leaving only the basket handles on the top half of the orange. Remove orange pulp between the basket handles.

4. Fill the basket with small flowers.

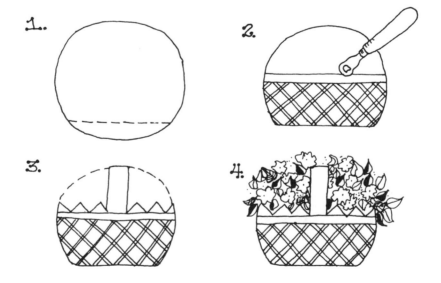

★ Fried Pastries with Cinnamon

Ingredients:

2 cups unbleached all-purpose flour

1 egg lightly beaten

¼ cup cold water

2 tablespoons granulated sugar

1 teaspoon vanilla extract

3 cups frying oil

Confectioners' sugar

Cinnamon

Method:

1. In a bowl add the flour, egg, water, granulated sugar and vanilla extract. Knead for a few minutes until a smooth, elastic, somewhat sticky dough is formed. Add more water if necessary.

2. On a floured surface roll out dough to about 1/8 inch in thickness or until the surface of the worktable can be seen through the dough. Cut into 1 x 3 inch rectangular strips.

3. Deep-fry in 3 cups of preheated 375-degree oil until golden brown. Drain pastries on paper towels, sprinkle with confectioners' sugar and cinnamon. For best effect, serve pastries while still warm or make ahead of time and heat pastries in a low-temperature oven then sprinkle with confectioners' sugar and cinnamon.

Lemon Mist Tea

Ingredients:

6 bags Lemon Mist tea

2 quarts water

Warm honey

Method:

1. Bring water to a boil in a glass pot. Remove from heat, add tea bags, let brew for a few minutes. Serve with honey on the side.

Menu 37

Sun Tea

Mama Es' Salad

Charcoal-Broiled New York Strip Steaks

Bowl of Fresh Fruit and Nuts

★ Chocolate Chip Cookie Concoction

Sun Tea

Ingredients:

8 tea bags

3 quarts water

Lemon wedges

Method:

1. Add tea bags to water in a large clear glass jar. Place outdoors in the sun for a day. Stir, remove tea bags and serve in tall glasses over ice with lemon wedges.

Mama Es' Salad

Ingredients:

2 cups peeled and grated carrots

4 cups unpeeled diced zucchini

½ cup dark raisins

½ cup sliced scallions

⅔ cup diced feta cheese

2 cups French Dressing (see recipe on page 64)

3 tomatoes sliced

2 purple onions sliced

Method:

1. Gently fold the first 5 ingredients with the French dressing at least 1 hour before serving. Place in a serving bowl and lay out alternating slices of tomato and purple onion around perimeter.

The Invincible Steak

On the night before their trial on the Colosseum floor gladiators ate meat to make themselves strong. In Sparta during the fourth century, if you were male and over twenty years of age, you were required by law to eat two pounds of meat a day. It was supposed to make you brave. It was only a few years ago that the modern-day gladiators and coaches insisted that athletes needed meat the night before the game. Of course, being more scientific, they referred to their training-table steak as protein. Then things changed.

The new message is that we needn't stop eating meat entirely. Instead, we should cut down our consumption and look to alternative protein sources such as fish, poultry, low fat dairy products, nuts, beans and seeds; hence -- less saturated fats -- lower levels of cholesterol -- a slimmer and healthier body.

Steak or any form of meat is still a good source of protein. It has delicious aroma and flavor and has texture unlike any foods derived from plants. Instead of eating the large eight or ten ounce steak, eat a smaller portion. A four or five ounce portion contains more than half the recommended daily allowance of required protein. At Maine Chance we serve a three ounce steak which still assures sufficient protein.

Charcoal-Broiled New York Strip Steaks

Ingredients:

6 5-ounce boneless loin steaks cut 1¼ inch in thickness

Your favorite seasoning salt or marinade

Oil

Method:

1. It is easy and fun to charcoal-broil steaks outdoors and, properly done, steak never tastes quite as good when cooked any other way. Before cooking the steaks have a uniform bed of charcoals with white ash showing. It is important to have an intense heat to sear the meat, trapping the juice inside, while giving the outside a crisp brown crust.

    Brush each steak with oil; place on well-heated grid about five inches above the flame. Steaks are best seasoned after or marinated before they are cooked. Seasoning with salt while cooking has a tendency to draw out the juices from the steak. Cook steaks on first side until the bottoms of the steaks are well browned. Turn steaks over with a spatula or a pair of tongs, and cook on the other side until desired doneness. A rare steak (all pink inside) when pressed quickly with the fingers will feel somewhat resilient. A medium steak (a small amount of pinkness left) will have less resiliency, and a well-done steak (no sign of pinkness) will feel firm. This touch method takes some experience. For a sure way of testing the steaks, make a small incision with a paring knife to check the inside. Some juice will be lost with this method. But it is better to check this way than to serve over- or undercooked steaks. As a rule, it is better to undercook than overcook steaks since you can always cook them a little bit more. Just in case you mess things up and cook the steaks past the point of no return -- enjoy your guests' company. It happens to the best of us!

Bowl of Fresh Fruit and Nuts

Ingredients:

Assorted fresh fruit

1 pound assorted nuts in their shells

Method:

1. Fill a bowl with a varied assortment of fresh fruit in season such as apples, oranges, grapes and bananas. Sprinkle nuts over fruit. Serve with nutcrackers, picks and bowls for nut shells.

★ Chocolate Chip Cookie Concoction
(serves 12 people)

Ingredients:

2 ounces bittersweet chocolate

1 12- to 14-inch oval platter

1 8-inch chocolate almond cake (see recipe on pages 84-85) or any other favorite chocolate cake

Kahlua or other coffee-flavored liqueur

½ gallon vanilla ice cream

1 ounce green creme de menthe

2 cups heavy cream

⅓ cup brown sugar

1 teaspoon pure vanilla extract

Approximately 1½ dozen Chocolate Chip Cookies (see next recipe)

Method:

1. Melt bittersweet chocolate and spread on wax paper with a spatula so that it is about ¼ inch in thickness. Refrigerate. When chocolate is hard, cut out C's using a 2½-inch round cutter (see diagram on next page). Set C's aside in refrigerator.

2. Line the inside of the oval platter with a 1-inch layer of chocolate almond cake. Sprinkle cake liberally with Kahlua.

3. Mound half of the vanilla ice cream (1 quart) in the center of the cake. Mix the creme de menthe into the remaining quart of ice cream. Spread this mixture over the mound of vanilla ice cream. Smooth mixture out with a spatula dipped in hot water and place platter in freezer as soon as possible.

4. Add the heavy cream, brown sugar and vanilla extract to a chilled whipping bowl. Whip until stiff peaks are formed. Refrigerate.

5. Just before serving take out prepared platter from freezer. With a towel soaked in hot water clean any melted frozen ice cream along the sides of the platter. Using a star tube and pastry bag (see Working with a Pastry Bag, page 204), pipe out a border of whipped cream along the bottom of the platter covering any exposed chocolate cake. Place the 4 C's monogram on a front side of the ice cream. Stud the top and sides of the ice cream with the Chocolate Chip Cookies and serve.

★ Chocolate Chip Cookies
(makes 5 dozen 2-inch cookies)

Ingredients:

1 cup unbleached all-purpose flour

1 cup whole-wheat flour

1 teaspoon baking soda

1 cup or ½ pound softened unsalted butter

½ cup granulated sugar

⅔ cup brown sugar

2 eggs

1 teaspoon vanilla

1 teaspoon salt

2½ cups bittersweet chocolate chopped into pieces

4 ounces bittersweet chocolate chopped into pieces

2 cups toasted slivered almonds (toast almonds in 400-degree oven for 10 minutes)

Method:

1. Preheat oven to 375 degrees.

2. In a small bowl sift flours together with the baking soda.

3. In a large bowl cream the butter and sugars together. Beat in the eggs one at a time. Add vanilla and salt. Gradually add flour mixture. Stir in the chocolate and nuts.

4. Using a 1-ounce scoop, a large spoon or a pastry bag, portion out cookies onto a nonstick or lightly greased baking pan. Bake approximately 12 minutes in 375-degree oven.

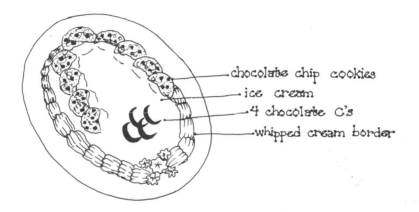

chocolate chip cookies
ice cream
4 chocolate C's
whipped cream border

On page 178 there is a misprint that I would like to bring to your attention. Under the ingredients for the chocolate chip cookie recipe it reads:

2 1/2 cups bittersweet chocolate chopped into pieces

It should have read:

2 1/2 cups packaged chocolate chips

Menu
38

Park Avenue Salad
(crabmeat, papaya and julienne cut celery)

Roast Duck with Blackberry Orange Sauce

Short Grain Brown Rice with Herbs
and Slivered Almonds

Buttered Whole Green Beans

★Amaretto Vanilla Ice Cream Crunch

Park Avenue Salad

Ingredients:

1 head Boston lettuce

8 ounces cooked shelled crab legs cut into 1-inch pieces

2 papaya, peeled, seeded and diced

1 stalk of celery cut into 1½-inch julienne pieces

Apple Belvedere Dressing (see recipe on page 72)

6 parsley sprigs

6 lemon wedges

Method:

1. Line 6 salad plates with a bed of Boston lettuce. Gently mix crab legs, papaya and celery with prepared dressing. Divide mixture among the 6 plates. Garnish with parsley and lemon wedge.

Roast Duck with Blackberry Orange Sauce

You are about to perform surgery. For the operation you will need a sharp knife and patience. Why surgery?

Duck has a hard time making the popularity chart because of its high fat content. Ask people what they think of duck, and the answer is usually, "I love it, as long as it isn't too fatty." If it were not for the extra fat, the poor duck would have a hard time staying afloat. This extra fat should not stand in the way of eating the delicious bird. If anything, fat has the advantage of keeping the meat moist and tender; kind of a built-in basting mechanism.

The best way to be sure your duck is not too fatty for your company is to remove the fat surgically after the duck has been cooked. I think you will find this method to be well worth the effort when your guests cannot understand how you make such moist duck with so little fat.

Ingredients:

2 5- to 6-pound ducks

Lemon juice

Salt and pepper

Oil

4 stalks celery chopped

1 onion chopped

4 carrots chopped

(ingredients continued on next page)

6 cups fresh or frozen orange juice

¼ cup Grand Marnier

¼ cup blanched julienne strips of orange peel

1½ cups fresh, frozen or canned blackberries

1 orange basket decorated with a fresh cut flower (see page 172)

2 cups watercress sprigs

Method:

1. Preheat oven to 425 degrees. Dry ducks thoroughly and season inside cavities with lemon juice and salt and pepper. Rub some oil on the skin of the ducks and on the bottom of a roasting pan. Spread chopped celery, onion, carrots, wing tips and duck necks on the bottom of the roasting pan. Place the ducks on their backs on top of the vegetables and roast in 425-degree oven for 20 minutes. Lower oven to 350 degrees and roast ducks for 20 minutes on each side. Roast ducks for the remaining 30 to 40 minutes on their backs. Remove ducks from roasting pan and set aside.

2. Drain off all the duck fat from the roasting pan and discard. Add 2 cups of orange juice to roasting pan. Place pan over burner and scrape up all of the browned pieces of vegetables and duck that may be sticking to the bottom of the pan. Take care not to scrape up any burned parts from the pan. Transfer the ingredients from the roasting pan into a heavy metal, non-aluminum saucepan. The saucepan should have the 2 cups of orange juice, the vegetables, wing tips and necks. Add the remaining 4 cups of orange juice; set saucepan on medium high heat, stirring occasionally, begin to reduce sauce to 2 cups of liquid.

3. Meanwhile, when ducks are cool enough to work with, remove back bones and add them to the saucepan. Cut ducks into quarters. Gently lift the skin away from the meat of the duck and scrape out as much fat as possible with a sharp paring knife. Take care not to pull and tear skin off of the duck pieces. Place skin back into its proper position.

4. When 2 cups of orange sauce are left in the saucepan, strain out and discard vegetables and duck pieces. Skim off any fat from sauce. Add Grand Marnier; bring to a boil; lower heat, cover saucepan and keep hot.

5. Arrange duck pieces skin side up on a 14- to 16-inch oval platter. Place platter in a 500-degree oven for a few minutes to heat up. Platters must be heat-resistant. If not, heat ducks on a roasting pan and transfer to heated platter. Spread prepared orange peel and blackberries over duck. Pour sauce over duck. Decorate the center of the platter with the orange basket. Place a few watercress sprigs around orange basket and on the two ends of the platter. Enjoy!

Short Grain Brown Rice with Herbs and Slivered Almonds

Ingredients:

4 cups strong-tasting chicken stock or canned chicken consommé (see Stocks -- Les Fonds de Cuisine, page 197)

2 cups short grain brown rice

2 tablespoons chopped parsley

2 tablespoons chopped chives

½ cup toasted slivered almonds (toast in 400-degree oven for 10 to 12 minutes)

Method:

1. In a skillet bring the stock or consommé to a boil, add rice, cover and cook over low heat for about 50 minutes until rice is tender but not mushy.

2. Mix in herbs and almonds. For a nice-looking arrangement, serve rice on one side of an oval platter with the string beans on the other side.

Buttered Whole Green Beans

Ingredients:

1½ pounds fresh green beans

½ cup water

1 teaspon butter

Salt and black pepper to taste

Method:

(see About Cooking Vegetables, page 200)

1. Wash and trim off the tips of the green beans.

2. In a skillet with a tight-fitting cover add the beans and water. Cover and cook over high heat for a few minutes, then uncover and continue to cook until all the water has evaporated and the beans are tender but still crunchy. This process should take about 7 minutes.

3. Add butter, salt and pepper, toss in pan for a few seconds and serve.

Amaretto Vanilla Ice Cream Crunch

Ingredients:

Vanilla ice cream

1½ cups coarsely chopped Oatmeal Raisin Nut Cookies (see recipe
  on page 133)

6 ounces amaretto liqueur

6 sprigs of mint

Method:

1. Place a scoop of vanilla ice cream in 6 dessert dishes or in 6 cham-
    pagne glasses. Spinkle with chopped cookies and pour over 1 ounce
    of liqueur. Garnish with a sprig of mint.

Menu
39

Justa Pasta Salad

Baked Filet of Sole or Flounder

Caper Sauce

Spinach Boats

Steamed Banana Squash

Peach Yogurt Parfait

Justa Pasta Salad

Ingredients:

1 cup elbow Vegeroni pasta (sold in most supermarkets and health food
   stores)

1 crookneck squash cut into ¼-inch slices

1 zucchini squash cut into ¼-inch slices

1 pint cherry tomatoes cut into halves

¼ cup sliced green onions

2 tablespoons pine nuts

French Dressing (see recipe on page 64)

Method:

1. In a large pot, bring 1 quart of water to a rapid boil. Add macaroni
    and cook al denté (still firm to the teeth) for about 6 minutes. Strain
    in a colander, run cold water over macaroni until cool.

2. In a bowl toss macaroni with remaining ingredients and serve chilled.

Cooking with Your Head in the Oven
or
How to Cook Fish Correctly

To cook fish correctly you must give it your undivided attention.
There is a very fine line between undercooked, correctly cooked, and
overcooked fish. This is especially true if you are cooking a thin filet,
which could take as little as two minutes of actual cooking time. Watch
closely. Have your head practically in the oven, broiler, or wherever you
are cooking the fish. Cook the fish until the meat is no longer translucent and when the flesh *just* begins to flake (separates when touched
with a fork). Once the fish is at this stage, any additional cooking time
will begin to dry out the fish. Cooked right, the fish will remain soft to
the touch and juicy, giving one a chance to taste the subtle natural oils
of the fish. By cooking in this manner, little added fat is necessary, except to prevent the fish from sticking to the pan or skillet and a touch of
butter or oil on the top of the fish to keep seasonings moist.

Baked Filet of Sole or Flounder

Ingredients:

6 5-ounce sole or flounder filets

1 tablespoon melted butter

Eight Seasons Salt (see recipe on page 55) or your favorite seasoning

Lemon wedges

Method:

1. Preheat oven to 375 degrees.

2. Lay out fish on a nonstick or lightly buttered baking pan. Brush with butter and sprinkle lightly with Eight Seasons Salt. Bake in oven for 10 to 15 minutes until fish just begins to flake. Serve with lemon wedges and Caper Sauce on the side.

Caper Sauce

Ingredients:

1½ cups Yogurt Mayonnaise (see recipe on page 83) or 1 cup yogurt mixed with ½ cup regular mayonnaise

¼ cup capers

1 tablespoon juice from capers

Skim milk or buttermilk

Method:

1. Mix all of the ingredients together. For a thinner sauce, skim milk or buttermilk may be added until desired consistency.

Spinach Boats
(makes twelve 3-inch boats)

Spinach boats can be made smaller and used for hot hors d'oeuvres. The spinach boats may be prepared ahead of time and kept frozen, ready to be used to suit many occasions.

Ingredients:

⅔ cup water

4 tablespoons butter or oil

½ teaspoon onion salt

⅔ cup whole-wheat flour

3 large eggs

⅓ cup whole milk

2 tablespoons unbleached white flour

¼ cup chopped shallots

1 tablespoon butter

1 cup whole milk

2 heads spinach, cleaned and chopped

(ingredients continued in next page)

¼ teaspoon salt

1/8 teaspoon cayenne pepper

12 whole almonds

Method:

1. Preheat oven to 400 degrees.

2. In a heavy saucepan bring to a boil the water, butter and onion salt.

3. Pour the whole-wheat flour all at once into the boiling mixture and cook the paste over low heat, beating it rapidly with a wooden spoon, until the ingredients are thoroughly combined and the mixture cleanly leaves the sides of the pan and forms a ball. Remove pan from heat and let cool for awhile.

4. Beat eggs one at a time into the mixture, beating well after each addition.

5. On a nonstick or lightly greased baking pan bag out approximately 2½-inch oval shaped shells using a No. 9 piping bit and pastry bag (see Working with a Pastry Bag, page 204). Bake at 400 degrees for 30 minutes until brown and crisp. Set pastry boats aside.

6. Mix the ⅓ cup of milk with 2 tablespoons unbleached white flour, making sure to have a smooth lump-free mixture.

7. In a saucepan, sauté the shallots in 1 tablespoon butter until soft and translucent. Add remaining cup of milk. While stirring, bring milk to a boil. Add prepared milk and flour mixture to boiling milk. Keep stirring while mixture comes back to a boil and thickens. Lower heat, simmer mixture for a few minutes and then remove from heat.

8. In a large kettle of boiling water, blanch spinach for one minute, then drain well by pressing down on spinach with your hands in a colander. Add spinach to milk mixture. Season with salt and cayenne pepper.

9. Cut and remove tops of baked pastry shells. Stuff each shell with spinach mixture and garnish top with an almond. Place prepared boats on a baking pan. Before serving bake in a preheated 400-degree oven for 15 minutes.

Steamed Banana Squash

The terms "summer" and "winter" for squash are confusing. "Summer" types are on the market all winter; and "winter" types are on the market in the late summer and fall as well as winter, and some are on the market all year. Generally speaking, the soft-shelled squash such as yellow, crookneck and zucchini fall into the category of "summer" squash, and the hard-shelled Hubbard, pumpkin and acorn are in the "winter" variety.

The banana squash, a winter variety, weighing from five to as much as seventy-five pounds is on the market August through March. Because of its large size it is most often cut and marketed in pieces. Banana squash has a delicate naturally sweet flavor and is easy to prepare either in pieces or as a purée. If you are concerned about having enough Vitamin A in your diet -- a mere half cup of banana squash as well as many other varieties of winter squash, will supply all the daily requirements.

Ingredients:

2 pounds banana squash

2 tablespoons water

Brown sugar (optional)

Method:

1. Preheat oven to 400 degrees.

2. Remove seeds and trim off hard shell with a sharp knife. Cut squash into uniform slices. Place in a casserole with a tight-fitting cover. Add 2 tablespoons water to bottom of casserole. Cover and bake at 400 degrees for about 40 to 50 minutes until a knife tip, when inserted into squash, comes out easily. Brown sugar may be sprinkled over cooked squash and then glazed under a broiler for added sweetness.

Peach Yogurt Parfait

Ingredients:

1½ cups frozen or fresh peeled chopped peaches

1½ cups plain yogurt

2 egg whites

2 tablespoons honey

6 large strawberries

Method:

1. Mix yogurt and peaches together. Beat egg whites with honey until stiff peaks are formed. Fold egg whites into yogurt/peach mixture. Distribute mixture into 6 parfait or other stemmed glasses. Garnish top with a strawberry.

Menu
40

Initialed Consommé

Roast Leg of Lamb with Mint Sauce

Diamonds and Potatoes

Spring Garden Vegetables
Simmered in White Wine

Confetti Fruit

Initialed Consommé

In what better way can you pay tribute to a guest of honor than by having her or his initials floating on top of the soup? On occasion, you may wish to use numbers rather than initials -- I floated the numbers "1981" on top of my consommé one year to celebrate the New Year's dinner.

These light, floating dumplings are made from the famous paté a chou batter. Paté a chou is most noted for making the shells for cream puffs and eclairs. However, this batter is so versatile that one can dream up a number of ways to use it. For example, large shells may be made that can be stuffed with turkey, chicken or crab salad. Or make very light cheese hors d'oeuvres by simply sprinkling grated Parmesan cheese over the piped out batter before baking.

Ingredients:

1 cup water

¼ pound butter

¾ teaspoon onion salt

1 cup and 2 tablespoons whole-wheat flour

1 cup or 5 large eggs

1½ quarts prepared consommé (For recipe see Consommé Parker, page 89. Follow steps 1 through 5.)

Method:

1. Preheat oven to 400 degrees.

2. In a heavy saucepan bring to a rapid boil the water, butter and onion salt.

3. Pour the flour all at once into the boiling mixture and cook the paste over low heat beating rapidly with a wooden spoon until the ingredients are thoroughly combined and the mixture cleanly leaves the sides of the pan and forms a ball. Remove pan from heat and let cool for a while.

4. Beat eggs one at a time into the mixture, beating well after each addition.

5. With a pastry bag and No. 2 pastry tube (see Working with a Pastry Bag, page 204) bag out initials on a nonstick or lightly greased baking pan. Bake at 400 degrees for about 15 to 25 minutes until golden brown and crisp.

6. Just before serving add baked initials to hot consommé.

Roast Leg of Lamb

"Stately" might very well be the word to describe a decorated leg of lamb surrounded by greens, a few fresh flowers and its high majestic shank bone wearing a silver crown. By the way, do you know what decorating a platter of roast leg of lamb is called? See answer at the end of lamb recipe.

Ingredients:

1 7- to 8-pound bone-in leg of lamb

2 tablespoons olive oil

3 large cloves garlic, mashed

1 teaspoon rosemary

1 teaspoon basil

1 teaspoon Dijon mustard

¼ teaspoon pepper

1 carrot chopped

1 onion chopped

2 stalks celery chopped

4 cups beef stock or beef consommé (see Stocks -- Les Fonds de Cuisine, page 197)

Assorted fresh herb sprigs such as watercress, parsley, rosemary, basil

A few fresh cut flowers

1 aluminum foil crown (see diagram, page 193)

Method:

1. Trim off as much visible fat from lamb leg as possible without cutting into the meat. Combine the olive oil, garlic, rosemary, basil, mustard and pepper. Place lamb in a shallow roasting pan. Rub the oil mixture thoroughly into the meat. Sprinkle chopped vegetables in bottom of roasting pan. Let lamb marinate at least 3 hours before roasting or refrigerate overnight if possible.

2. Preheat oven to 350 degrees. Insert a meat thermometer into the thickest part of the leg without touching the bone. Roast for approximately 2 hours until meat thermometer reaches 150 degrees. This will produce a leg of lamb slightly pink in the center. Remove leg of lamb from pan and let rest ½ hour before carving.

3. In the meantime, add stock to roasting pan. Place pan over burner and scrape up all of the browned pieces of vegetables and lamb that may be sticking to the bottom. Transfer the vegetables and stock to a saucepan. Cook for ½ hour until liquid is reduced to 2 cups. Discard vegetables and skim off fat from top. Set gravy aside and keep h o t .

4. Leg of lamb may be carved ahead of time in the kitchen or at the table. Set leg of lamb on a large oval platter with the shank bone extended upward. Cut a slice off the bottom side of the leg and use it as a wedge, if necessary, so that the leg of lamb will rest on platter without toppling over. To carve ahead of time, cut out a large piece of meat to the leg bone (see diagram). Cut meat into uniform slices and place back onto leg bone. Garnish platter with bouquets of parsley, watercress and mint. Place a few flowers behind the shank bone and cover the bone with aluminum foil crown. Pour hot gravy over lamb before serving.

Aluminum Foil Crown

1. Crumple a 24-inch piece of aluminum foil with your hands.
2. Fold foil in half lengthwise. With a pair of scissors cut 1-inch strips three-fourths into the folded side of the foil.
3. Roll foil up and staple at uncut end of foil.
4. Open strips of foil to form crown.

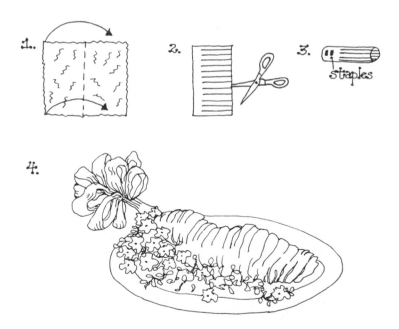

What is decorating a platter of leg of lamb called?
"Lambscaping"

Mint Sauce

Ingredients:

¾ cup white wine vinegar

2 tablespoons granulated sugar

1 tablespoon mint leaves, finely chopped

½ tablespoon green creme de menthe

Method:

1. In a saucepan, bring the vinegar and sugar to a boil. Remove from burner. Add mint leaves and creme de menthe. Serve on the side in a small pitcher.

A Tribute to the Potato!

You might say the potato has suffered a "bum rap." People watching their waistlines have aimlessly put the potato out of their lives; making the poor spud a culinary fugitive. But let's look at the facts. The potato is a low-cost natural food that is abundantly available throughout the year. One medium-size potato contains no more calories than a large apple. Potatoes are highly digestible; allergic reactions produced from eating them are extremely rare. Potatoes are a fair source of vitamins B1 and C and, in addition, have abundant content of iron, phosphorous, potassium and other minerals.

Unfortunately, because of traditional ways of cooking and serving, the potato is forced to keep company with the wrong circle of friends. Potatoes are french-fried, home-fried, baked with butter and sour cream, boiled and served with parsley and butter, fried into chips, and blended with mayonnaise for potato salads. Here lies the nemesis -- too much oil, butter, sour cream and mayonnaise.

So, who is responsible for this culinary dilemma -- the potato or the people? Let us free the potato and let it come out from being underground. Serve your potato with other whole foods such as milk and yogurt. Or, if you prefer, use the butter and oils sparingly. After all, I wonder what would happen if a calf were to drink only cream instead of whole milk from its mother. I believe the farmer would have to build a bigger barn.

Diamonds and Potatoes

Ingredients:

3 large uniform baking potatoes

¼ cup whole milk

¼ cup plain yogurt

¼ cup fresh chopped chives

2 strips well-cooked bacon, chopped

Salt and pepper to taste

Paprika

1 green pepper

Method:

1. Scrub potatoes clean. Pierce potatoes with a fork and bake in a 400-degree oven for about 60 minutes until potatoes are cooked soft to the touch. Let cool.

2. Slice a small piece of potato off the ends and cut each potato in half along the width.

3. Scoop out pulp leaving about 1/8 inch pulp on potato shells. Mash pulp and mix with milk, yogurt, chives, bacon, salt and pepper.

4. Stand the 6 potato shells on the sliced off ends on a lightly greased baking pan. Stuff potato mixture back into shells using a pastry bag with a star tube (see Working with a Pastry Bag, page 204). Potato mixture should be easy to squeeze out of bag without being runny. If it is difficult to pipe out, add more milk or yogurt to mixture. Sprinkle potatoes lightly with paprika.

5. Cut six 1-inch diamonds out of the green pepper and place diamonds on top center of stuffed potatoes.

6. Bake in 450-degree oven for 20 minutes before serving.

Spring Garden Vegetables
Simmered in White Wine

Ingredients:

4 carrots

2 stalks of celery

1 medium turnip

1 cup white wine or dry vermouth

1 tablespoon butter

(ingredients continued on next page)

½ teaspoon salt

¼ teaspoon white pepper

Chopped parsley

Method:

1. Julienne the vegetables by cutting them approximately 2 inches long and ¼ inch wide and ¼ inch thick. Vegetables must be cut as uniformly as possible in order to make this dish most attractive.
2. In a skillet with a tight-fitting cover, mix the wine, butter, salt and pepper. Cook vegetables, covered, one at a time. Remove each vegetable when done and set aside. The celery will take the longest time to cook and the turnip will take the least amount of time.
3. When all 3 vegetables are cooked, reduce liquid to a syrupy consistency. Before serving put all the vegetables back in skillet to reheat in syrup. Sprinkle lightly with chopped parsley.
4. To serve attractively, place spring garden vegetables in the center of a large oval or round platter and serve the heated, stuffed baked potatoes around the outside of platter.

Confetti Fruit

Ingredients:

1 cup ½-inch diced honeydew melon

1 cup ½-inch diced pineapple

1 cup ½-inch diced peeled apple

4 red glacé cherries cut into thin slivers

½ cup ½-inch dried apricots or dried peaches

6 whole strawberries or Bing cherries

6 sprigs of mint

1 small bottle of champagne or sparkling cider

Method:

1. Mix the melon, pineapple, apple, glacé cherries and dried fruit together.
2. Distribute mixed fruit into 6 dessert glasses. Top each mound of fruit with a strawberry or cherry and a sprig of mint. Pour 1 ounce of champagne over fruit and serve.

Related Reading

Stocks -- Les Fonds de Cuisine

No one understood how Grandma made such delicious soups and gravies that had flavor, aroma and body. If you asked Grandma, she would shrug her shoulders and say, "Oh, you just take a few vegetables, a chicken, some herbs, fill the pot with water and cook it until the chicken is tender." But let's see what she really did. For her famous chicken soup she didn't just use a few vegetables, she used *lots* of vegetables. She used a fresh chicken with its long neck. She used the gizzard and the feet. She added her favorite herbs and filled the pot with water that barely covered the ingredients in the pot. A very crowded pot with plenty of fresh ingredients -- that is what makes good chicken soup; that is what makes good sauces; that is what makes good cuisine.

All great chefs agree that good stock is the foundation on which almost all soups, sauces, stews, rice dishes and other fine dishes are built. "Stock is everything in cooking," wrote Escoffier. "Without it, nothing can be done." The French call stocks, "les fonds de cuisine," the basic liquids or, more exactly, the foundation of fine cooking.

Stock is derived from long, slow cooking of meat, bones, aromatic vegetables and a group of herbs known as the "bouquet garni." In the case of Grandma's chicken soup, she was actually making a chicken stock. Then by adding some rice or noodles along with a touch of seasoning she finished her stock and called it chicken soup.

Years ago all restaurant kitchens as well as household cooks made their own stocks. It was common to see a large stock pot sitting on the back of the stove full of bones and vegetables. When the roast was cooked and sliced the trimmings went into the pot. The tops of the tomatoes, leftover pieces of carrots and mushroom stems went into the pot.

Stock-making is not as popular now as it used to be. Many restaurants as well as household cooks use prepared canned soups and gravies. Or, they use canned chicken or beef consommé in place of homemade stock.

To a great extent it is no longer easy to prepare one's own stocks.

197

With chicken and meat cut into pre-packaged portions and the use of frozen prepared entrées, the beef bones, the long chicken necks and chicken feet so essential to making good flavored stocks are shipped out to the commercial soup companies. However, where there is a will there is way. To make beef stock, ask the butcher to save the bones for you before he ships them out. To make chicken stock, backs and wings can be purchased at a reasonably low cost if the necks and feet are not available. The other important ingredients, the vegetables and herbs, are always available.

In the recipes throughout the book I have called for either chicken and beef stock or canned chicken and beef consommé. Canned beef and chicken broths can also be used. Beef and chicken bouillon in cubes and packages are not a good substitute. They lack body and flavor and often have a tendency to make the dishes too salty.

The following are the recipes for beef, chicken and vegetable stock.

Beef Stock

Ingredients:

3 pounds beef and/or veal bones

4 onions, chopped with skin on

4 carrots chopped

4 stalks celery washed and chopped

1 bay leaf

½ teaspoon thyme

10 peppercorns

1 bunch parsley

1 clove garlic

Enough water to cover ingredients

Method:

1. Arrange bones and vegetables in a roasting pan and brown in a 400-degree oven for 30 minutes. Check to make sure that the vegetables do not burn.
2. Combine all of the ingredients in a large pot and simmer over gentle heat for about 6 hours. Skim off and discard any foam and scum as it rises to the top.
3. Strain the stock, discarding the vegetables, herbs and bones.
4. Use immediately or let cool a while, then cover and refrigerate. Before using, remove congealed fat from surface.

Chicken Stock

Ingredients:

Substitute chicken wings, necks, stewing fowl and other chicken parts for the beef and veal bones

Method:

1. Omit step 1 and continue as for beef stock.

Vegetable Stock

Ingredients:

Use same ingredients as for beef stock except leave out bones.

Parsnips, mushrooms, leeks, scallions may also be used.

Avoid the use of strong flavored vegetables such as broccoli and cabbage.

Method:

1. Omit step 1 and continue as for beef stock.

All stocks may be reduced in a thick-bottomed saucepan over a high heat until they reach the consistency of a heavy syrup, at which time they are poured into small containers, cooled and kept in the refrigerator. As their condition (once refrigerated) is solid, they will keep for weeks or, if frozen, for months. When additional flavor is needed for a soup, gravy or stew, add a few teaspoons of this thickened stock referred to by the French chefs as "glace de viande."

About Cooking Vegetables

Much has been said about the proper way to cook vegetables, especially concerning nutritive losses.

Boiling

The popular French method of cooking vegetables, especially green ones, has been to boil them in a large open kettle and then to quickly submerge them into cold water to prevent overcooking. This method has been criticized because much of the water-soluble nutrients can be lost in the boiling water. However, with a little kitchen ecology in mind, the cooking liquid along with the lost nutrients may often be used for the base of a good soup stock or sauce.

Steaming

Because the vegetables are not cooked directly in water, the steaming process favors retention of water-soluble nutrients. Most vegetables cooked by this method require a longer period of time than when boiled. Care must be taken to distribute the vegetables so that they cook at an even rate. If not watched properly this method may cause color loss in many green vegetables and may result in greater vitamin destruction than boiling.

Stir-Frying

The Chinese method of stir-frying vegetables in a small amount of oil and then covering with a lid to cook them in steam helps minimize nutrient loss. Cooking in a wok, both efficient and fun, is the most popular method used to stir-fry.

Baking

Some vegetables such as yams, potatoes, tomatoes and egggplant cook well and have little nutrient loss by simply baking with dry heat in the oven.

Microwave Cooking

The microwave oven is a fast, excellent device to use when cooking vegetables...it ensures good nutrient retention provided you're familiar with its cooking techniques.

My advise is to use any cooking method you prefer as long as you purchase the freshest vegetables possible and take care not to overcook them. If the vegetables are still crisp, naturally tasty and colorful, you may rest assured that the vegetables are still highly nutritious.

About Preparing Salad Greens

For interesting salads, use different varieties of greens rather than just one type when making most salads. Each green contributes a different color, texture and taste. Generally speaking, the darker the green, such as spinach, the more nutritious it will be. Quality and price are often most favorable when the different kinds of produce are in season in your area and are in bountiful supply.

To prepare salad greens, tear off any bruised leaves and discard. Tear or cut the remaining leaves into bite-size pieces and wash in a sink filled with plenty of cold water. After careful washing, the greens should be drained well in a colander. Remove the greens from the water rather than the water from the greens. This allows the grit and dirt to settle to the bottom of the sink and not back into the greens. After draining and removing as much water as possible by patting with a dry towel, cover the greens with a damp cloth or plastic wrap, or in a canister with a tight-fitting lid and refrigerate.

To Make Grade "A" Soufflés

There certainly is something very appealing about a well-made soufflé. It is light and airy. The inside is moist with a crunchy exterior. It forms a large crown way above the rim of the soufflé bowl, making it fit for a king or queen.

To make grade "A" soufflés -- soufflés that rise well above the bowl and continue to maintain their well-formed crown so one need not rush to the table before they fall --keep in mind the following suggestions:

1. Do not overbeat the egg whites. As soon as the egg whites begin to form stiff peaks, beating should be halted. Any further beating will have an adverse effect on the height and stability of the soufflé.

2. "Folding" the egg whites into the sauce base is just what the term implies. The idea is to maintain as much egg white volume as possible. By gently folding rather than beating the egg whites into the sauce, maximum volume is maintained. Folding may be done with a rubber spatula or with your hands. If you enjoy getting your hands into light oozy textures as I do, folding by hand is the only way to go. First, stir a big spoonful of egg whites into the sauce base mixture to lighten it. Then with your fingers stretched out and open, mix in the remaining egg whites by gently rotating your outstretched hand up and around the bottom of the bowl. Fold until the last trace of egg white disappears.

3. The most important tip, rarely mentioned in cookbooks, to help produce a worthy soufflé is to bake the souffle in a pan of water. The water needn't be more than ½ inch in depth. Not only does the water keep the soufflé moist, it will help it to maintain its structure while in the oven, on the table and even on the tip of the fork right before it meets its destiny.

Working with a Pastry Bag

The proper use of a pastry bag is a valuable attribute for the accom-plished cook as well as the professional chef. Pastry bags and various piping tubes are used for decorating cakes, making a variety of pastries, stuffing foods, bordering work, and a host of other functions. Nobody can deny the enticing beauty of a well-decorated wedding cake. Cookies can be made in one quarter of the time it takes to spoon them out by quickly piping the batter through a pastry bag. And, would the Coquilles Saint-Jacques ever have become so famous, if it were not for the decorative uniform waves of the bordering Duchess Potatoes?

Working with a pastry bag is simple and fun. Skill comes from careful pressure control -- the squeezing and relaxing of pressure on the bag. With smooth coordinated movements, simple rosettes and borders can be made that will add another dimension to your cuisine.

Pastry bags come in a number of sizes and are measured by the length of the bag. A No. 12 bag or twelve-inch bag is a good all-purpose size. Vinyl is considered to be the best material for pastry bags. It costs more than canvas bags but lasts longer, is easier to clean, and does not weep.

Pastry tubes come in many sizes and shapes for many different uses. Some tubes are used for just one purpose such as either making roses or leaves. The two most popular are the plain round piping tube and the star tube. The plain piping tube is used for stuffing foods, piping out cookies, making cream puffs and eclair shells, writing "Happy Birth-day," and for other various functions. The star tube is used for making rosettes, border work, and many other fancy designs.

With a pair of scissors, cut the end off of the pastry bag so that the tip of the pastry tube will protrude about halfway out of the bag. Open the end of the bag and cup it over your left hand (if you are right handed), forming a mouth. Spoon ingredients to be piped out into the pastry bag making sure it is no more than two-thirds full. Transfer bag to right hand. Twist and close the bag between your index finger and thumb. Hold finger and thumb securely to ensure that the ingredients will not back out when pressure is applied. Remember, the fingers of your left hand do the guiding and your right hand squeezes the bag.

Make rosettes by holding the tip of the pastry tube perpendicular over the item to be decorated. Squeeze, raise the bag slightly up and release pressure. Let your left hand guide the tip of the tube to the next position. Squeeze, raise the bag slightly up and release pressure.

To make borders, hold the tip at a 45-degree angle. Continue to squeeze while guiding tip up and down or straight across with your left hand.

Practice by piping out plain shortening onto cake pans, mixing bowls or wax paper. The more proficient you get, the more you will enjoy using a pastry bag. After a while, plain iced cakes can be transformed into tantalizing chef d'oeuvres. It's like learning how to paint with a brush after you've only done finger painting.

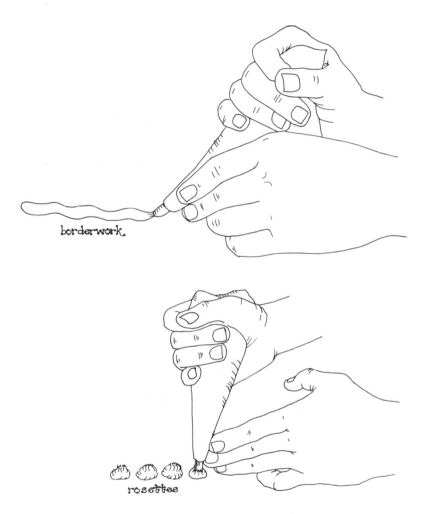

borderwork.

rosettes

To Order More Copies

Golden's Kitchen

This title can be ordered directly at *$19.95, plus $2.00 per book* postage and handling. There is no charge for postage and handling on orders of five or more books. All orders must be prepaid, check or money order, made payable to GOLDEN'S KITCHEN. Every effort will be made to send your book as soon as possible.

Mail to:

GOLDEN'S KITCHEN
2811 East Calaveros Drive
Phoenix, Arizona 85028